Ageism

at Magee

RETHINKING AGEING SERIES

Series editor: Brian Gearing
School of Health and Social Welfare
The Open University

'Open University Press' *Rethinking Ageing* series has yet to put a foot wrong and its latest additions are well up to standard . . . The series is fast becoming an essential part of the canon. If I ever win the lottery, I shall treat myself to the full set in hardback . . .'

Nursing Times

Current and forthcoming titles:
Miriam Bernard: **Promoting health in old age**
Simon Biggs *et al.*: **Elder abuse in perspective**
Ken Blakemore and Margaret Boneham: **Age, race and ethnicity: A comparative approach**
Julia Bond and Lynne Corner: **Quality of life and older people**
Joanna Bornat (ed.): **Reminiscence reviewed: Perspectives, evaluations and achievements**
Bill Bytheway: **Ageism**
Anthony Chiva and David F. Stears (eds): **Promoting the health of older people**
Maureen Crane: **Understanding older homeless people**
Mike Hepworth: **Stories of ageing**
Frances Heywood *et al.*: **Housing and home in later life**
Beverley Hughes: **Older people and community care: Critical theory and practice**
Tom Kitwood: **Dementia reconsidered: The person comes first**
Eric Midwinter: **Pensioned off: Retirement and income examined**
Sheila Peace *et al.*: **Re-evaluating residential care**
Thomas Scharf *et al.*: **Ageing in rural Europe**
Moyra Sidell: **Health in old age: Myth, mystery and management**
Robert Slater: **The psychology of growing old: Looking forward**
John A. Vincent: **Politics, power and old age**
Alan Walker and Tony Maltby: **Ageing Europe**
Alan Walker and Gerhard Naegele (eds): **The politics of old age in Europe**

Ageism

BILL BYTHEWAY

OPEN UNIVERSITY PRESS
Buckingham · Philadelphia

Open University Press
Celtic Court
22 Ballmoor
Buckingham
MK18 1XW

email: enquiries@openup.co.uk
world wide web: www.openup.co.uk

and
325 Chestnut Street
Philadelphia, PA 19106, USA

First Published 1995
Reprinted 1995, 1997, 2001

A catalogue record of this book is available from the British Library

ISBN 0 335 191754 4 (pb)   0 335 19176 2 (hb)

Library of Congress Cataloging-in-Publication Data
Bytheway, Bill.
    Ageism / by Bill Bytheway.
        p. cm. – (Rethinking ageing series)
    Includes bibliographical references and index.
    ISBN 0-335-19176-2   ISBN 0-335-19175-4 (pbk.)
    1. Ageism.   2. Ageism – Great Britain.   3. Age discrimination – Great Britain.
    4. Aged – Service for – Great Britain.   I. Title.   II. Series.
    HQ1061.B98   2000
    305.26'0941—dc20   94-27686
                                                                              CIP

Typeset by Type Study, Scarborough
Printed in and bound Great Britain by
Biddles Ltd, www.biddles.co.uk

To my mother, Phyl

Contents

Series editor's preface

The rapid growth in ageing populations in this and other countries has led to a dramatic increase in gerontology. Since the mid-1970s, we have seen a steady growth in the publication of British research studies which have attempted to define and describe the characteristics and needs of older people. Equally significant have been the very few theoretical attempts to re-conceptualize what old age means and to explore new ways in which we think about older people (e.g. Johnson 1976; Townsend 1981; Walker 1981). These two broad approaches which can be found in the literature on ageing – the descriptive (what do we know about older people) and the theoretical (what do we understand about older people and what does old age mean to them) – can also be found in the small number of postgraduate and professional training courses in gerontology which are principally intended for those who work with older people in the health and social services.

Concurrent with this growth in research and knowledge, however, has been a growing concern about the neglect of ageing and old age in the education and basic training of most workers in the health and social services, and about inadequate dissemination of the new information and ideas about ageing to lay carers and a wider public. There is, therefore, a widening gap between what we now know and understand about ageing and ageing populations and the limited amount of knowledge and information which is readily available and accessible to the growing number of professional and voluntary workers and others who are involved in the care of older people.

The main aim of the 'Rethinking Ageing' series is to fill this gap with books which will focus on a topic of current concern or interest in ageing. These will include elder abuse, health and illness in later life, community care and working with older people. Each book will address two fundamental questions: What is known about this topic and what are the policy and practice implications of this knowledge?

An understanding of ageism is central to comprehending ageing and what it is to be old in this society. In one sense ageism is like two other ideologies with which it is often compared, sexism and racism. All three ideologies depend on prejudice which serves to justify forms of inequality. Following Foucault we can say that they are all discourses through which forms of control and subordination are exercised. However, there are also ways in which ageism differs from the forms of oppression associated with gender and race. As Kathleen Woodward has pointed out we all have an interest in representations of ageing and the ageing body: age necessarily cuts across all our lives in the way other differences do not, so the analysis of age must be different from the analysis of race or gender (Woodward 1991).

Yet there is a curious paradox here. Old age is something we will all experience, but it is still much less discussed than racism or sexism and receives less opprobrium than prejudice based on sexual difference or physical impairment. As Bill Bytheway notes in this book, as a matter of everyday transaction we produce, buy and send birthday cards which contain flagrantly ageist messages: an example of just one of the taken-for-granted practices of ageism in our society. It is hard in 1994 to conceive of racist or disablist jokes being accorded the same benign acceptance. Why is ageism so unremarked, yet so prevalent? Is it because it involves a denial of our own ageing, a fear of personal old age which leads us to treat older people as, somehow, 'a race apart', different from ourselves or what we can bear to think we might become? Whether or not this is the explanation, it is important that age is added to the recent debates on difference. This book does just that and in a provocative and penetrating way which should also engage the reader and his or her beliefs and fears about old age. Not only does it review the literature on ageism, place it in a historical context and review current ageist practices in a wide range of settings, it also reconceptualizes ageism in its personal, institutional and cultural forms.

Bytheway also points to current work which is seeking to replace negative representations of ageing with others which accept or celebrate age rather than seeking to deny or disguise it. One example of such work in an area where ageism has had great impact concerns the Hen Co-op; six women, aged between 60 and 75, who have explored new possibilities by attempting to break out of the cultural restraints on the lives of older women (The Hen Co-op 1993). Their book, *Growing Old Disgracefully*, which records their experience through personal accounts, letters and poems, testifies to ways in which resistance to ageism can be both personally liberating and an inspiration to others. They achieve this through honest self-disclosure, courage and humour, rather than by presenting themselves as exemplars or standard bearers for a new movement. Surely, this is to be welcomed. As Bill Bytheway observes, we do not need even more role models telling us how we should behave in later life. But what we do need to see demonstrated much more publicly through the mass media are the many varied and individual ways in which people grow old and live ordinary but satisfying lives.

If, as Woodward suggests, the negative representations of old age are partly due to its association with physical decline and death, then they will be difficult to change. But a first step in this work is for gerontologists and others to challenge the ageist assumptions and associations in our language and culture. Like those older people who are changing our consciousness of what old age can be about, this book contributes to that process of re-definition by deepening our understanding of ageism and old age.

Brian Gearing

References

The Hen Co-op (1993) *Growing Old Disgracefully: New Ideas for Getting the Most out of Life.* London, Piatkus.

Johnson, M. (1976) That was your life: a biographical approach to later life, in J. M. A. Munnichs and W. J. A. van den Heuval (eds) *Dependency and Interdependency in Old Age.* The Hague, Nijhoff.

Townsend, P. (1981) The structured dependency of the elderly: creation of social policy in the twentieth century. *Ageing and Society,* 1, 5–28.

Walker, A. (1981) Towards a political economy of old age. *Ageing and Society,* 1, 73–94.

Woodward, K. (1991) *Ageing and its Discontents: Freud and other Fictions.* Bloomington and Indianapolis, Indiana University Press.

Acknowledgements

This book has developed out of Unit 2 of the Open University course *An Ageing Society* (K256). Particular thanks go to the course team: Brian Gearing, Julia Johnson, Caroline Malone, Sheila Peace and Robert Slater; also to Moyra Sidell, Joanna Bornat, Mary Horrocks, Malcolm Johnson and Eric Midwinter, all of whom provided invaluable encouragement and help in the development of that unit and this book. Gilly Crosby of the Centre for Policy on Ageing assisted in the library research.

I am particularly indebted to Andrea Thomas who kindly agreed to my including some quotations from interviews she undertook in 1993 with receptionists, nurses and other health care professionals. These came from her postgraduate research project concerning patient participation in primary health care which she undertook whilst working for Teamcare Valleys.

I am also indebted to Ken Blakemore, Mary Scally, Ann Allen and Ros Bryar, colleagues in Swansea, who have regularly offered timely advice and encouragement; to Nigel Stott, Professor of General Practice, University of Wales College of Medicine, who was responsible for my employment while much of this book was being written; and finally again to Julia Johnson who, several years ago, helped me recognize the peculiar complexity of ageism and who has frequently helped me think through some of the issues.

We are especially grateful to the following for their permission to reproduce photographs and pictures in this book: Mo Wilson, Cardiff; Format, London; Roger Davies, University of Wales Swansea; Hirwaun Primary School, and *The Guardian*.

PART I

The origins of ageism

This book is a review – a review of what I have read about ageism, and of some of my ideas about this peculiar form of social oppression. It is not a comprehensive cataloging of all the different forms of ageism, nor is it an exposure of the poverty, humiliation and misery that 'the elderly' are made to suffer. The primary objective is not to prove that ageism exists but rather to clarify what it is. As I argue in this book, ageism is not discrimination by dominant groups in society against one particular minority group; it is much more complex than that. So the primary objective is to clarify the issues involved in order to conclude with a coherent understanding of this neglected social phenomenon.

Although I have described it as a review, the book is also designed as an aid to teaching. If the worlds we live in are to become any less ageist than they presently are, it is critical that students should be on their guard regarding matters of age. And so the book includes a number of case studies. These are separate from the main text and might be used for group discussions. I have also appended an annotated list of further reading which I would recommend to students.

As a review of the literature on ageism the book is intended to be a contribution to gerontological research. There is a strong case for arguing that gerontology has reinforced rather than challenged ageism. Some gerontologists may argue that their research has been objective and neutral and, as such, has challenged many of the myths about ageing. But, as I shall demonstrate, the conceptual frameworks and the terminology of such research are often wholly compatible with those of ageism.

I have attempted to ensure that the review is up-to-date, but I have also drawn heavily upon material published some time ago. It is, of course, a consequence of modernism that one is inclined to be apologetic about out-dated material. For example, several of the works I draw upon use the universal masculine but I have resisted the urge to take appropriate editorial action. The relationship of the idea of out-dated material to ageism should be obvious.

Perhaps I should declare at the outset that, as I write this, I am aged 51, and am white, male, able-bodied, heterosexual and employed by a university. This gives me a particular perspective on life, the significance of which I would like to think I do not underestimate. In my view this does not disqualify me from addressing issues of gender, race, etc. However, I recognize that I am not best placed, for example, to offer a full history of the impact of feminism on our understanding of age. In any case, this is a book about ageism and anti-ageist action, not about how age is involved in other forms of prejudice and discrimination. This may sound a little like splitting hairs, but it is all too easy for the examination of ageism to become dominated and constrained by a concern with other more visible issues that are placed higher on the politico-cultural agenda.

I am particularly sensitive, of course, to the question of age. Some would argue that I am far too young to understand the power of ageism in the lives of people in their seventies and eighties and that the battle against ageism should be led by those of pensionable age. Perhaps I am, and perhaps I should have waited. However, I have been an active member of the British Society of Gerontology since its founding in 1971. For a long time now, I have been eager to get started on a book about ageism. Here it is.

What is ageism? The first chapter is a general introduction to the concept. It begins with four examples and ends with a working definition. Ageism is as much to do with us and our age as with any minority group from which we might feel safely distant.

The second chapter provides an account of how age has been conceived and measured in other societies, in particular in ancient Greece. This demonstrates that current ideas about age and old age are based upon a model of the ageing process that has a long pedigree. Historically this has exerted great power in the intervening centuries and is at the root of modern ageism. The model fosters the development of attitudes to age which, it is argued, has led to the repeated involvement of age in debates about euthanasia. Despite the distance of the ancient Greek philosophers, it is hoped that the intimate connection between their view of life and current threats to the lives of older people will be apparent.

The third chapter in this scene-setting first part focuses on ageism as a social construct itself. It is important to note that, although it is clearly apparent that most societies are essentially ageist, a critique of this simple fact is not possible without an appropriate terminology, and the word 'ageism' itself is essential. It was Robert Butler who introduced the word into popular discourse in the late 1960s. Some of those espousing positive anti-ageist attitudes to old age since then, however, have been powerful agents in the promulgation of ageism.

The fight against ageism is not conducted solely on paper and it would be all too easy to overlook the efforts of many who have sought to challenge ageist institutions and to expose the oppression that older people are suffering. And so I conclude this first part of the book with an account of some of this political action.

1

Introduction: Too old at 58

Ageism is about age and prejudice. But it is not simple. It appears in all sorts of situations and affects people of all ages. In this chapter I have attempted to develop the basis of a working definition. First, however, here are four examples of prejudice based on age.

Prejudice based on age

Five-year-olds

In a court case in 1992 Oldham and Bexley Councils rejected applications for accommodation made by two homeless five-year-olds. 'It is manifestly absurd to suppose that a five-year-old can make an application', said counsel for the councils. Lawyers for the boys argued that they were entitled to apply for housing in their own right as 'persons' under the 1985 Housing Act (*The Guardian*, 28 March 1992).

These two comments contrast the presumed absurdity of claims for the competence of a five-year-old and the assertion of the age-less rights that come with personhood. Is it not ageist to imply or presume that the basic moral rights that come with personhood should be conditional upon age?

Industrial workers

The following is an extract from an interview I undertook with a steelworker who was made redundant in 1980 at the age of 58 from the Port Talbot steelworks in South Wales.

I began going down to the Job Centre enquiring about a job, something like driving. I was told that there was no chance: 40, you know, over 40. 58, something like that I think I was, and I was completely discouraged from even attempting to look for a job, but I did apply then for a course, a course as a brickie. I thought I could get a little bit of a trade there. I was invited to take the written test which I passed. Then I had to go for a practical test and there were four of us in this practical test and, out of the four, I was the only one that they said was capable of going on to do the course. So later on then, I was taken to the office. Whether it was then that they looked at my documentation or not, I don't know but they got quite a little bit alarmed to think that I was 58 years of age, you know, and even the instructor turned to me. He said, 'Oh,' he said, 'if I'd known that,' he said, 'I'll have to put you on concrete blocks.'

'Well,' I told him, 'I got no fear of handling concrete blocks. I've done it before when building my own walls.' And then he went on to say that they didn't realise that I was as old as that and the fact that I passed the test . . . I would be hearing from them in a couple of weeks. But they told me then that they would be keeping a very close eye on me during the course. So I felt then that pressure was being put on me. When I came to think about it, I thought I don't intend to have that, I've never had it all my working life, I don't want anybody standing and watching me over my shoulder. I mean my record will stand for itself. So I wrote back then and I told them that, after due consideration, I didn't intend to have that type of pressure put on me. Therefore, I suggested that they give the vacancy to some younger person, you know, and that's how that came to an end.

This man's commentary is powerful evidence of how chronological age can be used negatively in the labour market. First he found that the staff in the Job Centre were completely negative about his age – put crudely, he was 18 years too old. He then found that, in seeking training, his age overruled his proven potential. It seems likely that there was an upper age limit on entry to the training course, and that the training officers were embarrassed to find that they had overlooked his age when allowing him to take the tests. Having made the mistake, they could only respond by threatening informal pressure – keeping a very close eye on him. As a result he backed out, defending his record and making way for a younger person. Imagine the sense of injustice that he must have felt as he set about phrasing his letter of withdrawal.

Hospital patients

There are many examples of the abuse of older people. Some focus specifically upon chronological age; others upon a person's position within an institution. Consider the following account of an observed incident in a long-stay hospital ward:

An old lady is wheeled from the ward bathroom to her bed area on a hoist, the seat of which is about four feet from the ground. She is inadequately covered and her bare buttocks hang through the commode-type seat so that her anus is exposed to view. Her bottom has not been dried and looks sore. She is weeping as she is wheeled along. While this scene is taking place, a clinical tutor from the associated Teaching Hospital is visiting the ward. She smiles as she greets the student nurses who are transporting the old lady in this fashion.

(Godlove *et al.* 1982: 53–4)

Age consciousness: an acute sense of our public image
Photograph: Mo Wilson

In this situation it is not the patient's age that is significant. Rather it is that the patients on this ward – all the patients – are 'geriatric cases'.

Carers

The fourth example of prejudice based on age comes from the information leaflet on benefits after retirement, issued by the Benefits Agency:

> What you earn does not affect your pension. If you earn enough, you will have to pay income tax.

> If you are sick or disabled and get benefit for personal care, the person looking after you (your carer) may be able to get Invalid Care Allowance.

For a carer to get benefit, you must be getting one of these benefits:

- Attendance Allowance;
- the middle or top rate of Disability Living Allowance for personal care;
- Constant Attendance Allowance if you are a war pensioner or sick or disabled from work.

Your carer must:

- not be a paid professional like a doctor or a nurse;
- be aged 16 to 65;
- look after you at least 35 hours a week;
- look after you at least 22 weeks in every 26 week period;
- not be in full-time work. They can work part-time as long as they earn less than a set amount after taking off expenses.

(Benefits Agency 1993: 20, 27–8)

These regulations indicate fairly clearly that people of pensionable age are allowed to gain income from employment but, unlike people under 65 years of age, they will be denied an Invalid Care Allowance if they find that employment is not possible due to care commitments.

This regulation reflects the presumption that people of pensionable age will not be undertaking care work other than the incidental help that might be fitted in with other activities. This flies in the face of all the evidence regarding the main sources of informal care in later life (see page 81). It also implies that people of pensionable age have no need of paid employment because they are in receipt of a pension. But, again, as we shall find on page 113, this does not follow. The decline in the value of the basic pension means that many people are obliged to seek income from other sources; often this is only possible from work that pays.

These four examples reflect the enormous diversity of ways in which ageism is evident in modern society.

Age revelations

How is age significant in our everyday lives? On the day that this is being written, there is a feature in the daily newspaper about the Dean of a threatened London Medical College. The journalist writes that she (the Dean):

was 50 last year ('Dreadful!' she shrieks) but has the energy and dynamism of someone at least a decade younger.

(*The Guardian 2*, 20 January 1993: 8)

It is worth asking what this statement represents. It includes two elements: the reported response of the Dean to reaching 50 – dreadful – and the journalist's assessment of the Dean's energy and dynamism – equivalent to a younger person's. There is no escaping the double message that the fiftieth birthday was not enjoyed and that energy and dynamism are associated with younger people.

Now listen to this exchange based on an interview by a researcher (*RA*) with two health centre receptionists (*SD* and *RM*):

RA: Can I be indelicate and ask your age?
SD: 41 I am.
RM: 26.
RA: Oh, there we are.
SD: She's showing off.
RA: Isn't she just!
RM: Put 21 for me.
RA: Put 21? No, 26 is young. I can't remember being 26 (laugh).

Note how the 'indelicate' question generates all kinds of comments: *SD* accuses *RM* of showing off; *RM* wants to lie; *RA* associates herself with *SD*, unable to remember being as young as *RM*; and so on until all three end up laughing.

So are we all sensitive to revealing our age? How self-conscious do we feel when asked outright how old we are? Do we shriek? Do we feel our energy ebbing? Do we feel uncomfortable as we stutter over the answer? Do we find ourselves elaborating it with comment about how we feel and what we do? Or do we feel comfortable about our age, willing and able to provide a direct and simple answer, seeing it as part of an ordinary biographical introduction? Or do we feel affronted because we fail to see how our age is relevant? Do we find ourselves wondering why we are being asked our age? Do we avoid answering it?

In addition to these personal responses – shrieking, laughing, bemoaning, denying, or whatever – our answer to the question can be used for more formal or bureaucratic purposes. Just like height, weight, IQ tests, number of children, health and income, age is a personal characteristic that can be measured on a standard scale. What then happens is crucial to understanding ageism. It is almost always included in application forms for benefits, jobs and services. In the processing of these forms, age is often set against age-specific norms and expectations as in the case of the steelworker. When we deviate from these norms, we may be applauded for being younger than we are – 'Fifty last year! You're acting like a 40-year-old. Aren't you wonderful!' – and, if needs be, regulations regarding age are overlooked. Or, the norms may be mobilized in order to put pressure, deny us resources, or channel us in particular directions – 'We'll be keeping a very close eye on you!'

Age in newspapers

Age figures in many different contexts. A real newspaper story reads as follows (names have been changed):

Brown, 45, was at the 'centre of the web' in a plot to cheat the City Council by dishonestly using highly confidential information, it was alleged. It was passed to him by Joe Green, 47, a committee chairman . . .

In the dock with Brown are ex-councillors Green and White, 49; and busi-
nessman John Grey, 45.

There is nothing particularly unusual about this story – again it appeared in a
newspaper that happened to be at hand at the time of writing – and the ages of
the defendants are unexceptional. None of the defendants are reported as
being appalled by or proud of their age. And their ages seem irrelevant to the
issue being reported – so why are they included?

Perhaps it is because the defendants' ages indicate that they are all of the
same middle-aged generation. Interesting – but significant? And surely not the
reason for their ages being reported. The answer is that including age is standard journalistic practice. And why? Because age conveys precise information
in the minimum of space (just two typographical symbols), information that
directly contributes to the construction of an image of the person being described.

But why is it not necessary to add the word 'years' after the two-digit numbers: 'Brown, 45 years, was at the centre of the web . . .'? How do we know
that Brown was 45 years of age and not 45 stones in weight? Because we all
know that age is typically reported in newspapers solely as a number: it has
become standard practice. In this sense it is part of the language, something
that we have to learn if we are to make sense of newspapers.

We also know that someone involved in such a newspaper story is quite
likely to be 45 years of age (and unlikely to be 45 stones in weight). If we had
read: 'Brown, 18, was at the centre of the web . . .', we would have been confused. Surely Brown was more than 18 years of age? Could he be 18 stone? But
why would the journalist report his weight? And wouldn't the journalist have
written: 'Brown, who weighs 18 stones, was at the centre of the web . . .'?

So it is convention backed up by expectations that ensures that we will
understand that the 45 refers to age. This simple argument indicates how important and pervasive age has become in the relationship between the individual and society. It is not you who has decided that age is interesting, so
interesting that you are going to ask everyone you meet how old they are. You
didn't ask the newspaper how old Brown, Green, White and Grey were. It
wasn't you who volunteered your age in a box entitled 'Other Relevant Information' when you applied for a bank loan. Rather it is the dominant values of
the society in which we live, values which have emerged over decades if not
centuries, that oblige us to be age-conscious and age-alert if we are to understand how to fill in forms and what we read in newspapers, and if we are to
sustain meaningful communication with the social institutions around us.

And it is because we have gained such a discerning knowledge of how people
behave at various ages that we in turn behave in an age-specific way. At 18 we
know we are not expected to attempt to cheat the City Council by using highly
confidential information. Most of us don't have such information when we're
18 and so we don't even think of cheating the Council – confirming expectations. Just as at 45 we don't even think of lying about our age in order to get
into the cinema, because we know that even the most youthful-looking 45-
year-old will be let in without a thought being given to age.

To summarize this argument: if we are to fully understand ageism, we have to appreciate the extent to which it is an age-specific society in which we live, and how we have all learned to be age-sensitive while not necessarily being age-conscious.

Ageism: just another 'ism'?

What is an 'ism'? How does ageism relate to sexism and racism? One answer is to assert boldly:

These are three philosophies that we find offensive and which we would expect ordinary, liberal, tolerant, intelligent people to be against.

Gauche though this may sound, it is nevertheless the basis of an understanding. We all know about racism and sexism don't we? And, because we all know we all know about racism and sexism, we have little trouble in talking about and being conscious of racist and sexist issues. The terms acquire meaning through usage and, when misunderstandings or disagreements arise, meanings are clarified by the exchange and analysis of examples, i.e. through further usage.

It is because we all know about racism and sexism, we have no difficulty in knowing what ageism is about. Ageism is prejudice on grounds of age, just as racism and sexism is prejudice on grounds of race and sex. Consider one choice example. An article in *The Independent* (9 January 1993: 39) is headlined:

Ageism takes off at British Airways

and the first sentence is, ' "Do airlines discriminate against older people?" asks Gladys Glascoe of North Thamesmead.' What is significant about this is that the word *ageism* only appears in the headline, and that it is defined implicitly in this first sentence as 'discrimination against older people'. The parallels with gender and race could not be clearer: take out 'older people' and put in 'women' or 'the ethnic minorities' and the headline would have had sexism or racism in place of ageism.

Let's suppose Gladys Glascoe is a doctor and had booked in advance. Let's consider the possibilities. There's no problem until she appears. First Dr Glascoe is a woman. 'Oh, I'm sorry. I thought you were a man. I'll just go and change this.' It doesn't matter what 'this' is, Dr Glascoe had been pre-judged to be a man.

Next, Dr Glascoe is black. 'Good afternoon, Dr Glascoe. Now, I'm afraid I have to fill in this form. Nationality?' Whereas had Dr Glascoe been white, the introduction might have been: 'Good afternoon, Dr Glascoe. Now, I'm afraid I have to fill in this form. Nationality, British?' Again Dr Glascoe had been pre-judged to be British.

Next is Age? – there it is on the booking form. Let's guess that Dr Glascoe was born in 1918 (Gladys Glascoe's age is not revealed in the article but she does refer to herself as an 'elderly lady'), and with her answer the booking clerk books her into a seat that is not next to an emergency exit. Why? Because it is British Airways policy not to book 'women of a certain age' into seats adjacent to exits for fear that they will not be able to use the emergency equipment and will block them in an emergency.

This, according to the article, is the ageism that was taking off and again we have a clear example of how people – or perhaps women – are pre-judged on the basis of age. Just as a 58-year-old man is thought incapable of managing concrete blocks, so a woman in her seventies is considered unable to use emergency equipment.

We have to accept then that this is how the word ageism is now being used in the media. As this example clearly indicates, ageism – a term that was first used as recently as 1969 – is becoming part of the vocabulary of the media in the 1990s. As such, the word itself is a phenomenon of growing significance which complicates our attempts to develop a sound understanding of the responses of society to age.

It would be easy to accept this kind of definition – ageism, equivalent to racism and sexism, is discrimination against old people – as the basis of this book and I could set about documenting many examples of such discrimination in considerable detail. There is little doubting that such discrimination does occur and so, at the outset, need we quibble about definitions?

Well, as the example of Oldham and Bexley Councils indicates, younger people are discriminated against, too and, as the example of the steelworker indicates, middle-aged people can find their age being used against them. Indeed, one sometimes has the impression in discussing ageism with people involved in employment policies that they perceive ageism to be no more than the unacceptable use of age in the processing of people in the labour market – when you suggest that it also affects very old people living in nursing homes, you are faced with looks of confusion and incomprehension. No matter what our age, there will be times when it is invoked to deny us things that we seek.

With rare exceptions, the way in which we are affected by sexism and racism has a degree of continuity throughout our lives. This does not apply to our experience of ageism. 'No one is born old'; 'We are all growing older from the day we are born'. Such aphorisms confirm the distinctive nature of age as a characteristic of the individual – one which, unlike gender and ethnicity, is constantly changing. It is the only progressive condition with which we all have to live. For these reasons alone, it is essential that we start from scratch; that we set sexism and racism to one side in the development of our understanding of ageism.

Sex and race, along with many other divisions within society such as class and disability, are issues relating to – but not determining – our experience of ageism. The belief that other dimensions are more important than age is a peculiarly clear indication of just how endemic and insidious ageism is. It is the kind of absurd value judgement that we are all inclined to make when we think of age as just another variable.

So, in the final section of this chapter, a working definition of ageism will be introduced which will underlie the writing of this book, a definition that will expand upon the popular conception of ageism as discrimination against old people. First, however, we need to consider in a little more detail the situation of younger people. Is this book about their experience as well as that of older people?

Ageism and younger people

The enormous public debate over voluntary abortion has tended to centre upon the concept of life rather than the more sociological concept of personhood. Is the human being to-be-born a foetus (i.e. a non-person) or a baby (i.e. a person)? In July 1992, for example, a Scottish court ruled that a baby in the womb is a person, reversing an earlier ruling that it was a foetus – not a person (*The Guardian*, 29 July 1992).

The denial of personhood is a peculiarly fundamental form of prejudice and it is experienced by younger people throughout the process preceding the acquisition of adulthood. Through the Children Act and before that the Homeless Persons Act, a number of important aspects of personhood have been aired in court, well exemplified by the case of Oldham and Bexley Councils.

Young people are often perceived to be threats to the dominant forces of social order (Cohen 1980). It was not difficult during the winter of 1993/94, for example, to hear the sounds of moral panic in the crisis that overcame the British media first, following the Tory Party Conference of 1993, over single parents and then over young criminals following the James Bulger case, in which a toddler was murdered by two young boys. The impact of these public concerns upon the views of the individual are well illustrated by the following statement made by a nurse who had been in practice for 23 years:

> A lot of the young people just have not got the ability to cope. A lot of them are single parents. Some have the back-up of their parents, others are trying and struggling on their own. I'm always appalled these days about how often you hear 'my social worker'. You know, the young people just accept that they need a prop.

By linking 'young people' to 'these days', the nurse is commenting upon the characteristics of a generation as it faces up to the responsibilities of adulthood, rather than upon an age group. The inability of young people to cope is associated not with the consequences of age but with the social circumstances of their time: by having access to a social worker they are being led into 'accepting that they need a prop'.

Ageist prejudice is based primarily upon presumptions, sometimes about chronological age and sometimes about different generations. It is by linking age to such presumptions – that 'five-year-olds' are incapable of making applications, and that 'young people' are unable to cope – that young people suffer from the ageist prejudice of their elders.

Early education

During our first 20 or so years of life, one of the dominant influences in our lives is the educational system, a system that is geared to a progressive annual cycle. In the fracas over the national tests in English for 14-year-olds being launched in 1993, for example, the School Examinations and Assessment Council admitted that the pilot trial was being taken by 15-year-olds not

14-year-olds. As a result of this 'blunder' the teacher unions were discussing a possible boycott (*The Guardian* 15 January 1993).

For many of us childhood is the only time in our lives when our social status and our social world changes systematically each year. The system of age-specific expectations is, potentially, enormously oppressive. The key element in this annual cycle of educational progress is encapsulated in the modest word *growth*. The contrast in our appearance at age 20 weeks and 20 years is immense and the dominant feature of this is size. Over the first 20 years of life, our body typically grows in weight from a few pounds to several stones, and in height from a few inches to several feet.

The social consequence of this is the constant revision of expectations and a near-universal consciousness and interest in the growth of the child: 'My! How you've grown!' is the kind of remark we all repeatedly suffer as we slowly progress towards becoming fully-developed adults. The pattern of growth has been studied in minute detail, not only by the more attentive members of the ordinary population, but also by acknowledged experts. Graphs of child development have been plotted almost since the day that graph paper was first printed.

Development relates not just to height and weight, but also to strength, speed, intelligence, school performance, and a host of other measurable characteristics. This has led to the establishment and refinement of clinical standards of growth; as a consequence, the comparative progress of children can be measured in precise detail. The 1960 Stanford-Binet Intelligence Test provides ample evidence of this. For example, it includes the following item:

> Vocabulary. Six-year-olds: 6 words should be defined correctly from the vocabulary list of 45 words. Eight-year-olds are expected to define 8, ten-year-olds 11, twelve-year-olds 15, and fourteen-year-olds 17. The word list consists of the following 45 words: orange, envelope, straw, puddle, tap, gown, roar, eyelash, mars, juggler, scorch, lecture, skill, brunette, muzzle, haste, peculiarity, priceless, regard, tolerate, disproportionate, lotus, shrewd, mosaic, stave, bewail, ochre, repose, ambergris, limpet, frustrate, flaunt, incrustation, retroactive, philanthropy, piscatorial, milksop, harpy, depredation, perfunctory, achromatic, casuistry, homonculus, sudorific, parterre. For the scorer, examples are given of good and bad definitions.
>
> (Terman and Merrill 1960)

On the basis of such scales, we might find ourselves being adjudged as having a reading age that is significantly different from our chronological age. As children we often sense that we are competing in this kind of educational race: at the time most of us know the rules and that due rewards come from success. Through this we acquire a sensitivity to the minutiae of age-specific expectations, a sensitivity which will survive to constrain much of our behaviour in later life.

Becoming adult

The ageist pressure to succeed in meeting and surpassing expectations continues right up to the time when we gain adulthood. But now, in addition to a tightly scheduled standard for growth, there develops further competition regarding the eventual outcome of our long training in personhood. Some come out with educational qualifications; others do not. Some end up marrying; others do not. Some find well-paid work; others do not. And the qualifications, spouses and jobs that are available and possibly obtained are often ranked systematically according to social prestige, enabling our successes to be publicly judged. The nineteenth-century writer John Symonds wrote in his diary:

> I am 21 today, the end and goal I have so often thought of. Up to this point I have been struggling, saying, 'When I am a man I shall do this, understand this, be great; now I am a boy, and from a boy little is expected.' The sum of intellectual progress I hoped for has been obtained, but how much below my hopes. My character has developed, but in what puny proportions, below my meanest anticipations. I do not feel a man. This book is an evidence of the yearnings without power, and the brooding self-analysis without creation that afflict me. I am not a man.
>
> (Brett 1987: 360)

This kind of failure, however, may be defined as a continuation of adolescence. At the point when our physiological growth ends and we become 'fully-fledged adults', there follow a wide range of expectations about adult social behaviour and responsibilities. However, we may not yet be fully trained, equipped or positioned in order to enter into adult careers in employment and family life. Students who hope to enter the medical or legal professions, for example, are required to undertake a long training of several years, with the result that paid employment and marriage is postponed. Some of us who fail exams (of whatever kind) or who are not offered jobs, are encouraged to re-sit them or to apply again. Some of us decide to explore the world before we settle down, or to save up before we marry. There are many ways in which the end of our pre-adult development may be fudged and settling into adulthood postponed.

Given this oppressive scheduling of the processes of gaining adulthood, small wonder that so many of us rebel! Far from being allowed to develop interests, knowledge, skills, occupations, associations and friendships that we freely choose ourselves, we are pressured from every direction into following well-worn paths (Franklin and Franklin 1990). 'Do this! Do that! And with a bit of luck and hard work you'll be successful and happy!' 'No thanks!' is the response of many.

What I would argue is that the ageism experienced by young people is the same phenomenon as that experienced by older people, but the experience itself is radically different. For this reason, the remainder of this book focuses primarily upon ageism in later life.

A working definition

There is something excessively didactic about attempting to coin 'the definitive definition' of a concept such as ageism. Nevertheless, it is important that I offer some understanding of what the term means to me when I use it.

I first became interested in ageism when Maggie Kuhn visited the UK in

1978. On television she demonstrated that ageism was something that was serious and, in the magazine, *New Age*, she defined ageism simply as 'discrimination against people on the basis of chronological age' (Whitehouse 1978). Shortly afterwards, I commented in the same magazine:

> It was the first article I had read which used the term in a serious and unqualified way.The term has often been used by others, but rather coyly as though the speaker feared the audience might think that a joke was being made.
>
> (Bytheway 1980: 29)

Three years later, I was asked to take part in a review symposium on the book *Vitality and Aging* (Fries and Crapo 1981). In working through this my initial concern was with the statistical analyses of the authors. I came to realize however that they were forwarding a thesis which implied that we were moving towards a society characterized by a 'long life of vigour and vitality ending suddenly, one day, on schedule' (1981: 135). Without anticipating it, I found myself concluding my review with the comment that Fries and Crapo were articulating 'a markedly ageist thesis'; that they were 'engaged in the construction of a biological basis for social discrimination between living people' (Bytheway 1982: 391). It was clear that their argument was preparing the ground for old-age euthanasia: for easing the rapid passage of those who appear to have reached the 'natural' end of their long lives. It was this that made me first appreciate the biological base and the potentially awesome power of ageism.

I collaborated with Julia Johnson on the organization of the 1988 conference of the British Society of Gerontology in Swansea and, through this, it became apparent to us that there was a continuing neglect of the concept of ageism, and this led to our formulating the following 'working definition':

1 Ageism is a set of beliefs originating in the biological variation between people and relating to the ageing process.
2 It is in the actions of corporate bodies, what is said and done by their representatives, and the resulting views that are held by ordinary ageing people, that ageism is made manifest.

In consequence of this, it follows that:

(a) Ageism generates and reinforces a fear and denigration of the ageing process, and stereotyping presumptions regarding competence and the need for protection.
(b) In particular, ageism legitimates the use of chronological age to mark out classes of people who are systematically denied resources and opportunities that others enjoy, and who suffer the consequences of such denigration, ranging from well-meaning patronage to un-ambiguous vilification.

(Bytheway and Johnson 1990)

2

Ugly and useless: The history of age prejudice

> People at the end of the life-cycle continuum have constantly been described as 'old'. Old age is an age-old phenomenon.
>
> (Achenbaum 1978: 2)

As I will argue in Chapter 9, this idea that old age has an age-old, universal and natural reality needs to be challenged. In this chapter, however, I will accept that it exists as a result of this popular way of thinking, and will review the history of some of the consequences, particularly in regard to ancient Greece. Much of this relates directly to 'old age' and 'old people', and I will forego the constant use of inverted commas. There is a growing literature on the history of retirement as a social institution (Graebner 1980; Walker, A. 1989; Laczko and Phillipson 1991). This is highly relevant to the question of age prejudice and I will draw upon some of this work in Chapter 7. In this chapter, however, I want to concentrate on age itself.

Looking back

The literature on the history of old age has tended to revolve around matters of number, household arrangements, poverty and the role of old people in society. It is difficult to document prejudice as such: for example, to establish the extent to which the institutions of past societies routinely pre-judged the circumstances, resources and needs of older people.

Perhaps we can accept the assumption that what is written in a particular period of history of a particular society does reflect ideals which are dominant and determine in large part the circumstances in which people live their lives. Historians, however, have gone to considerable lengths to gather data which challenge contemporary beliefs about the position of older people in the past (Fennell *et al.* 1988: 27). In particular there has been a major effort to dispute

An image of the past. This wartime photograph is of a day room for women in a residential home (Samson, 1944: 31). The caption reads: 'Neat uniform and good surroundings do not always compensate women for the loss of private possessions which give that "homely touch".'
Photograph: Unknown

the positive image of a past in which older people were valued and respected. For example, Stearns asserts:

> We can grant immense problems for the elderly at the present time, but we do not have to assume that their lot has ever been strikingly good in Western society . . . The old have consistently been treated unkindly in Western culture.
>
> (Stearns 1977: 20–1)

Who holds a rose-coloured image of the past? Oddly enough, this is an under-researched question. From experience, however, we know that politicians are inclined to articulate and draw upon this tendency: John Major's 'Back to Basics' campaign is a good example. In part, politicians are reflecting a popular yearning but, conversely, they are actively disseminating and strengthening the belief that human values in the past were better than they are now. But, perhaps the people who believe that life was better in the past, who are most significant for a study of ageism, are not politicians but those older people who have suffered from ageist discrimination If, as we age, we are made to feel unwanted, useless and out-dated, then it is inevitable that we will look back nostalgically to those times when we were wanted, useful and felt bang up-to-date. We will believe that in those days we respected our seniors in a way that no longer applies. And it is inevitable that if we now feel cut off from other forms of social activity, then when we get together with our age-peers we will bemoan the present state of affairs. And, of course, when politicians join in by articulating these same thoughts more publicly, the more gullible of us will be the more inclined to give them our vote.

Most of us have had experience of these kinds of discussions. Periodically we find ourselves jumping to the defence of youth when the older generation mounts what seems to be an unfair attack. What they say about younger people seems prejudiced and ignorant and, in stark contrast, what they say about life when they were young sounds like pure make-believe: a travesty of the truth that we – the defenders of youth – have gained from our own study of the history of the twentieth century. For example, we feel we have discovered the truth about what happened in Bloomsbury or Munich or Hollywood or the General Strike from the exciting and challenging work of younger historians. When we then read the nostalgic autobiographies and worldly reviews of the more famous of the surviving members of the older generation, we are liable to reach for pen and paper in order to challenge the promulgation of their dangerous 'myths'.

When we look to professional historians for an understanding of the significance of old age in the past, however, we need to remain sceptical. First, many of their sources are the same as described above – the words of the established, powerful and famous, many reflecting personal anxieties about later life rather than changing cultural values and institutional regulations. Second, historians are in business with their publishers, and they do good business paradoxically, not just by challenging what they perceive to be widely held but invalid beliefs, but also by adopting uncritically other popular assumptions and terminology. So, when books are given challenging titles such as *Old Age in a New World* we should not expect the author to give much attention to evidence that suggests that old age might not actually exist in the New World.

What I am arguing here is that we should view all accounts of the history of old age with a degree of scepticism. Much of it is bound to be coloured by the authors' experiences of, and involvement in, the ageism that is intrinsic to the society within which their books are written and published.

Chronological age

As argued in the previous chapter, the measurement of age is critical to the study of ageism. In modern western society, age is measured primarily according to the annual cycle and in particular through the birth certificate and the celebration of birthdays. This has been characteristic of many earlier societies. For example, Minois (1989: 19) quotes Herodotus in demonstrating how precise the ancient Persians were:

> Of all days in the year a Persian most distinguishes his birthday and celebrates it with a dinner of special magnificence. A rich Persian on his birthday will have an ox or a horse, or a camel, or a donkey baked whole and served up at table, and the poor some smaller beasts.

In many societies longevity is perceived to be a form of divine blessing – 'God save the Queen! Long live the Queen!' This hope, however, can complicate the business of recording and enumerating age. On the evidence of the Old Testament, at 969 years Methuselah was the 'absolute record holder for longevity in Western culture' to quote Minois, and Abraham, Ismael, Isaac, Jacob and Joseph all passed the century mark, averaging a life span of 150 years between them (Minois 1989: 28).

Age was also measured numerically in Greek society but rather more plausibly. Minois lists the length of life of 48 eminent Greek philosophers (1989: 55–6). These statistics are interesting. A single number is offered for 30 of the 48 – ranging from 53 (Eudoxus) to 98 years (Zeno) – and two or more numbers for seven others (e.g. Democritus: '100 or 109 years') reflecting, we might suppose, multiple and inconsistent records. Twelve of the 30 single numbers are multiples of ten – statistically we would expect only three and so this indicates a degree of rounding. Of the eleven philosophers whose numerical length of life is not given, eight died when they were 'old' or 'very old', two died at an 'advanced age' and one in 'extreme old age'. No one is described as having died prematurely or when 'middle-aged' and so it is possible that these were the eleven who, for one reason or another, left the world of philosophy, perhaps retiring to the mountain village from which they came, and whose eventual deaths went unrecorded.

What this suggests is that, while there was an arithmetic consciousness in the world of the Greek philosophers, there was also a degree of latitude which permitted rounding, estimating, inconsistencies and forgetting. Whatever the reason, this data indicates that terms such as 'old' and 'advanced age' are themselves measures of age: Xenocrates, for example, was 82 years when he died, whereas Xenophon was of advanced age.

How then did the Greeks decide who was 'old' or of 'advanced age'? Pythagoras suggested that old age started at 60, whereas for Plutarch it started at 50. However, old age, although anticipated on the basis of chronological age, was also associated with health, well-being and status. Consider the words of Mimnermus in the seventh century:

> Happy they who die at the age of 60, since once painful old age has arrived, which renders man ugly and useless, his heart is no longer free of evil cares, and the sun's rays bring him no comfort.
>
> (Minois 1989: 47)

This clearly indicates that old age does not arrive before 60 – it is expected at some unspecified time thereafter – and that it is *old* age not age which 'renders man ugly and useless'. Little wonder that, with this in prospect, death in the comfort of the sun's rays and free of evil cares was to be welcomed!

In many past societies, it was only the most privileged who had the mathematical and literary skills to keep an accurate record of their date of birth and age. People were judged on their public appearance and this reflected health, gender, status and age – but only according to broad categorizations. In Britain, it was only with the establishment of parish registers that most people came to know exactly how old they were (Thomas 1977: 207). The need to measure age numerically developed in the nineteenth century as the law increasingly focused upon the institutional control of individuals according to age.

The length of life was usually measured in the Middle Ages by dividing it up into stages. A stage can be defined as a period in life, loosely related to age, characterized in distinctive ways, and being part of a succession of stages that covers the whole of prospective life from birth onwards. In this way the set of stages provides not only a division of the life course but also a basis for categorizing the population according to age.

The stages of life

The stages of life have a long history. They were often represented by visual images published in broadsheets, church windows, woodcuts, engravings and paintings (Cole 1992). This powerful imagery, often linked to religion, is the basis of rigid cultural expectations about behaviour and appearance. Along with its accompanying vocabularies, the stage model is still used extensively today and, as a direct consequence, it has considerable power in structuring our lives and the way we think. For example, Thomas comments:

> Of all divisions in human society, those based on age appear the most natural and the least subject to historical change. The cycle of infancy, youth, maturity and decline seems an inexorable process.
>
> (Thomas 1977: 205)

Thomas might think that this division is the least subject to change but there is considerable variation in the number of stages into which life has been presumed to be divided. Cole (1992: 5) describes how ancient authors tended towards three, four (as in Thomas's proposition), or seven stages (as in Shakespeare's *As You Like It*), but that as many as twelve have been postulated.

This way of accounting for the ageing process has always been popular in the study of age. In the 1930s, for example, on the basis of analysing 400 biographies, Frenkel-Brunswik (1968) identified five distinctive phases. In the post-war period Erikson (1980) has developed a theory that has become particularly well-established in psychological gerontology. It postulates eight stages outlined as an epigenetic chart, in each of which the individual is struggling to resolve two contrary dispositions. However, although listed according to age, Erikson does not conceive of his eight stages as constituting a sequence through which the ageing individual actually passes:

> The epigenetic chart also rightly suggests that the individual is never struggling only with the tension that is focal at the time. Rather, at every successive developmental stage, the individual is also increasingly engaged in the anticipation of tensions that have yet to become focal and in reexperiencing those tensions that are inadequately integrated when they were focal; similarly engaged are those whose age-appropriate integration was then, but is no longer, adequate . . . At each successive stage, earlier conflicts must be reresolved in relation to the current level of development.
>
> (Erikson *et al.* 1986: 39–40)

What this suggests is that those who propagate stage models, think of them as no more than models that represent a certain idealized life course. Often it is little more than a device for structuring a book. For example, even though he describes the divisions as arbitrary, Nicholson has titled his book *Seven Ages*, attaching chronological ages to each of the seven as a rough guide (1980: 22).

A question that is rarely considered when stages are introduced is whether or not there is a hierarchy of divisions. In many societies there is a primary distinction between children and adults, one to which the distinctions between infants and schoolchildren and between the old and the not-old, for example, are secondary. Adults are then usually subdivided, separating the mature from the declining (to use Thomas's terms), or the old from the not-old. During the twentieth century this division has become strongly associated with retirement from paid work, with the receipt of pensions and with the state of dependency. This pattern of associations, all reflecting the structure of society as much as the capacities and needs of the individual, has become the basis of the theory of structured dependency (Townsend 1981) and, more generally, of what is referred to as the political economy of old age (Phillipson and Walker 1986).

In contemporary gerontology, following the lead of Neugarten (1974), there has been much acknowledgement of the contrast between the 'young-old' and the 'old-old'. The terminology itself implies unambiguously that this is a division of 'the old'. Strenuous efforts, however, have been made over the last 20 years to establish a new stage: the third age. This movement reflects a trend towards earlier retirement and an earlier release from parental responsibilities, as much as a distinction between the young-old and the old-old. Effectively the third age is fusing the later part of non-old adulthood and the active, younger, part of old age (Banks 1992). Significantly the numerical basis of the term

---

Shakespeare's seven ages

You might like to look up Jaques' speech in *As You Like It* (Act 2, Scene 7). Nicholson (1980) has articulated doubts about the validity of this speech:

> I was impressed by the fact that the seven ages of man had such a distinguished historical pedigree, and felt that Shakespeare's ac-count of them still strikes a chord which the modern ear has no difficulty in recognizing. But it was the same speech in *As You Like It* which planted in my mind a doubt about the theory of the adult life-cycle, a doubt which grew larger the longer the project lasted. It occurred to me that the sequence Shakespeare described – infancy, schooldays, courtship, military service, magistracy, retirement and second childhood – could never have applied to more than a tiny fraction of the population, specifically upper-class males.
>
> (Nicholson 1980: 19)

Apart from the depressingly negative and well-known image of the last scene 'sans everything', Shakespeare was also offering the idea that life is made up of seven pre-determined acts, each characterized by an entrance and an exit on to the world's stage.

implies that the division between the second and the third is on a par with that between the first and the second, and that it is the second stage (not the third of Thomas's sequence) that corresponds most closely to the period of working life. Both Neugarten and the proponents of the third age (Laslett 1989: 77) have argued against definitions based on chronological age. Despite this the Carnegie Inquiry into the third age, for example, defines it 'for statistical purposes' as 50 to 74 (Banks 1992). Laslett (1989: 4) refers to the fourth age as a period of 'final dependence, decrepitude and death' and it is clear from his argument that entry into this age is part of his new mapping of life. It is on this that Young and Schuller part company with him:

> Elevating the third [age] by the comparison is only done by treading down the fourth. The labelling problem is wished on to even older and more defenceless people.
>
> (Young and Schuller 1991: 181)

Rise and fall

Cole (1992: 18–19) argues that in the sixteenth century there was an ideological shift from a life circle, in which an angel holds together the beginning and the end of life, to the rise and fall of a two-sided staircase. Typifying the latter, he describes the 1540 woodcut by Jorg Breu:

> On a bridgelike stepped arch, ten personifications of the ages of man are seated. Beneath are animals that traditionally symbolized each age. Behind the apex of the arch, the figure of Death turns to shoot his arrows toward the ascending side of the bridge. On that side, the sky is naked and clear. But on the side where the elderly men sit, the sky is dark and cloudy – an allusion to the evening or winter of life. Beneath the arch, Breu engraved a scene of the Last Judgement, with John the Baptist and the Virgin Mary pleading for the souls of the faithful.
>
> (Cole 1992: 19)

All stage models have since entailed a degree of rise and fall. Sometimes the metaphor of the hill is used rather than the staircase. 'You're over the hill' is a classic ageist put-down; a particularly clear statement of this model is provided by Leonard Williams, a doctor writing in 1925:

> When a man reaches the crest of the hill on his earthly pilgrimage he finds himself on a plateau. He may be said to reach the crest of the hill at the age of 30. As things now are he has attained to the far end of the plateau by the time he is 45, and when he has reached 50 he is usually well on his way down a rapidly falling slope.
>
> (Williams 1925: 37)

The common assumption in all these symbolic representations is that, as we pass through the stages of life, we initially rise by acquiring a full range of human resources and skills. After a period of time we begin to descend through the final stages. The model underlies basic political assumptions about employment: the plateau corresponds to that part of life during which one is either engaged in paid work or expected to be actively seeking such employment. A third way of conceptualizing the model is through reference to the domestic household and to the powers, rights and responsibilities of 'the middle generation' upon whom younger and older generations are perceived to depend. Regardless of the way in which we interpret the rise and fall of life, however, the significant point is that we are making positive and negative judgements about many aspects of age.

Recognition of this multi-faceted evaluation of the quality of life during the middle age plateau is provided by Bromley:

> Middle age does not refer to the earlier stage of life when people in competitive achieving societies are making their way through successive occupational levels and establishing a network of family members and lasting friendships; nor to the later stage when they are preparing to disengage from their main occupational role. So, in some respects, middle age is a high point in the life-cycle. Most people then are in fairly good health; their psychological capacities are relatively unimpaired; they have accumulated considerable experience which they can use to advantage; they are usually as well off, secure and privileged as they are ever likely to be. The physical vigour of youth may have passed or the supposed tranquillity of old age not yet arrived, but overall 'middle age' compares favourably with other ages, and is indeed sometimes referred to as the 'prime' of life.
>
> (Bromley 1988: 159–60)

Where Bromley's careful argument fails is in the presumption that people engaged in competitive achieving societies necessarily succeed in making their way through a career, establishing a network of family members and lasting friendships, and in reaching a position where they are able to prepare to disengage from their main occupational role. It is because these expectations are so powerful, so powerful indeed that they become the basis of academic disciplines, that so many suffer from a sense of failure when life diverges from this scenario. Bromley acknowledges that it is only *most* people who are in fairly good health in middle age; their psychological capacities are only *relatively* unimpaired; and they are *usually* as well off, secure and privileged as they are ever likely to be. Regrettably, however, he does not detail the ageing experience of those who deviate from these ideals.

Ambivalence towards older people

Under the rise and fall model, the extremes are valued more negatively than the middle period. However, although old age is represented by the slippery slope, we are often taught that this stage is associated with power and wisdom. This ambivalence towards old age has been a key issue in the historical study of old age. Historians have sought to assess the extent to which old age and older people are respected or rejected within a particular society, valued or feared.

Some have argued that the problem reflects the social heterogeneity of those over a certain age. If it is true that the rich get richer and the poor get poorer, then it follows that with age we grow more different: some richer, some poorer; some more respected, some more rejected; some more valued, some more feared:

> Both today and throughout history, the class-struggle governs the manner in which old age takes hold of a man: there is a great gulf between the aged slave and the aged patrician, between the wretchedly pensioned ex-worker and an Onassis.
>
> (de Beauvoir 1977: 17)

The Greek philosophers, uninterested in the view or experience of the aged slave, were inclined towards making broad generalizations from their privi-leged positions, and tended to view old age as a curse. Some, such as Plato and Cicero, challenged this, arguing strenuously that old age had its compensations – not least that of allowing one to engage in earnest philosophical discourse undistracted by the trials and tribulations of earlier adult life. These contra-dictory views became the substance of many debates and differences. Minois, having studied them in detail concluded that:

> While some preferred suicide to an excessively advanced and decrepit old age, most of them were preoccupied with the problem of a great age: they talked about it frequently in their works and even dedicated whole treatises to it . . . It is revealing that none of these wise men state whether old age is in itself a good thing. All these old men only accept their age for as long as it is accompanied by health . . . The philosophers, like other people, did not suffer old age gladly. When they looked at it objectively, their opinion was more subtle but never very favourable . . . Most of them concurred in recognizing that old age is a defect: it resembles everything that decays, and youth everything that grows, as Pythagoras said . . . Of course, old men had to be honoured, as Chilo and Pythagoras demanded. And of course the Stoics taught that one's parents must be honoured immediately after the gods. But, on the whole, the philosophers were muddled about old age, which brought them more torments than it did prestige and wisdom.
>
> (Minois 1989: 54–7)

His main conclusion concerning this ambivalence came down on the side of the negative. Society allows the old only one role: unfailing wisdom. If they fail in this, as they almost inevitably must, then they are condemned to exclusion and vilification (Minois 1989: 303).

This has to be viewed with some scepticism: it reflects a generalized societal view of the old which confuses fears of one's own old age with attitudes to older people. As I suggested at the beginning of this chapter, historians such as Minois are heavily dependent upon the words of a small privileged group who, through the status they have gained in life, are prone to grand sweeping generalizations. They are not independent and unbiased observers: Plato at 80 is able to see the modest pleasures of old age to which the fearful Aristotle at 50 is blind.

Nevertheless, it is quite clear from Minois' research that the Greek philosophers had a strong sense of the existence of old age and of old people in the population. The same was true of the Romans, and the linguistic legacy of these two cultures has been to sustain the concept of 'old' in many subsequent societies.

Obviously old age was a critical element in any conception of future existence that incorporated an afterlife. The rewards and penalties attached to specific behaviour came to colour the prospects of one kind of afterlife or another:

> During the Middle Ages, the ages of life found their way into the repertoire of a new army of mendicant friars, who urged the lax Christian folk to turn from their wicked ways.
>
> (Cole 1992: 13)

Christianity developed 'a rich tapestry of astrology, humoral pathology, and natural philosophy' in explaining the connections between stage, death and sin (Cole 1992: 10). The following, for example, included in a Presbyterian funeral service in America in 1841, is a good illustration:

> The decay of age, as of death, is the sinner's accomplishment. Every old man, therefore, presents in his body the testimony of nature to SIN and DEATH.
>
> (Cole 1992: 88)

Age and achievement

The following is a choice example of ambivalent reasoning about the strengths and weaknesses of age. Writing in the booming years of the 1950s, the years of 'modernization', Lehman was concerned to inform policies on education and training about how the development and dissemination of knowledge is affected by age.

> Whatever the cause of growth and decline, it remains clear that the genius does not function equally well throughout the years of adulthood. Superior creativity rises relatively rapidly to a maximum which occurs usually in the thirties and then falls off slowly. Almost as soon as he becomes fully mature, man is confronted with a gerontic paradox that may be expressed in terms of positive and negative transfer. Old people probably have more transfer, both positive and negative, than do young ones. As a result of positive transfer the old usually possess greater wisdom and erudition. These are invaluable assets. But when a situation requires a new way of looking at things, the acquisition of new techniques or even new vocabularies, the old seem stereotyped and rigid. To learn the new they often have to unlearn the old and that is twice as hard as learning without unlearning. But, when a situation requires a store of past knowledge then the old find their advantage over the young.
>
> (Lehman 1953)

Trying to map these various rises, falls and transfers in creativity, wisdom, ability to acquire new techniques, rigidity and learning capacity, each against age, is an interesting exercise. How important have these kinds of claims been in setting the basis for age prejudice?

Euthanasia and age

Given such views about mortality and age, it would be surprising if age were not a consideration in the debate about euthanasia. The concept of a dignified death has drawn much from our beliefs about distant societies:

> The Eskimo, whose resources are meagre and most uncertain, persuade the old to go and lie in the snow and wait for death; or they forget them on an ice-flow when the tribe is out fishing; or they shut them into an igloo, where they die of cold.
>
> (de Beauvoir 1977: 59)

The Eskimos were not alone. Herodotus cited examples of tribes in the Caucasus and India that killed those of advanced age. Those who, at that point, were in good health were then eaten. de Beauvoir reviews a wide range of ethnological evidence and notes that: 'Very poor tribes, and especially very poor nomadic tribes, practice both infanticide and the killing of the aged' (1977: 96).

The case of the Eskimos is, for many of us, part of the common knowledge that we have acquired as curious children brought up in modern Western society. The demise of the aged Eskimo is shrouded by the image of the noble savage stoically accepting a dignified death. Eskimos, nomads, savages – they all evoke the image of a primitive and archaic way of life. This kind of knowledge about distant societies has a legendary quality, not unlike the knowledge to be gained from the Bible. It seems totally disconnected, for example, from the modern world of occupational pensions and community care.

Nevertheless, euthanasia is a highly topical issue in the 1990s and references to 'the elderly' often figure in the debate. Although much couched in terms of terminal illness, voluntariness, living wills and so on, the mere fact that age figures at all implies a certain continuity: in all societies there are expectations regarding age, the value of continuing life and the manner and timing of death.

One of the most infamous incidents was that of the speech of the English surgeon Sir William Osler when retiring from Johns Hopkins Medical School in 1906. Graebner has provided a detailed account of the resulting furore. He argued that it supported his own argument that:

> a society that is dedicated to progress and allows its economic institutions to define its terms must learn to sacrifice the older generation for the younger.
>
> (Graebner 1980: 53)

This is not dissimilar to the observation of de Beauvoir regarding very poor tribes noted above. Laslett (1989: 98) has suggested that Graebner took the proposal of Osler too seriously; that Osler's views were extreme even in 1906. Graebner argued, however, that Osler represented a developed ideology committed to furthering efficiency and productivity – that he was engaged in

> the effort to organize a creative tradition in science: to make systematic the emergence of intellects hostile to system, routine and tradition.
>
> (Graebner 1980: 8)

In the cause of progress the defenders of tradition had to be sacrificed.

A peaceful departure through chloroform

The following is an extract from the speech given by Sir William Osler in 1906:

> I have two fixed ideas . . . The first is the comparative uselessness of men above 40 years of age . . . It is difficult to name a great and far-reaching conquest of the mind which has not been given to the world by a man on whose back the sun was still shining. The effective, moving vitalizing work of the world is done between the ages of 25 and 40 – these 15 golden years of plenty, the anabolic or constructive period in which there is always a balance in the mental bank and the credit is still good.
>
> My second fixed idea is the uselessness of men above 60 years of age, and the incalculable benefit it would be in commercial, political and in professional life if, as a matter of course, men stopped work at this age . . . In that charming novel, *The Fixed Period*, Anthony Trollope discusses the practical advantage in modern life of a return to this ancient usage, and the plot hinges upon the admirable scheme of a college into which at 60 men retired for a year of contemplation before a peaceful departure through chloroform. That incalculable benefits might follow such a scheme is apparent to any one who, like myself, is nearing the limit, and who has made a careful study of the calamities which may befall men during the seventh and eighth decades. Still more when he contemplates the many evils which they perpetuate unconsciously, and with impunity.
>
> (Graebner 1980: 4–5)

How many successful and famous people have approached their retirement in this way, looking back with bitterness at the obstacles that older people have tried to put in their way, preferring a fixed period of isolated contemplation to a continuing battle with the 'calamities' of real life?

Having commented upon Osler, Laslett goes on to cite the eminent biologist, Sir Peter Medawar, and Donald Gould, a medical journalist, as two people who have raised the issue of euthanasia and older people. Although keen to stress the not-too-serious irony of these writers, Laslett makes the telling comment:

> Someone not too far away from this 75th birthday can perhaps be forgiven for asking what would happen if anyone so much as ventured to refer in passing to a holocaust of all black people in conversation with such persons as Medawar and Gould, let alone print and publish remarks to this effect.
>
> (Laslett 1989: 99)

Age bars on medical treatment

It is clear that current concerns with euthanasia and age are far more serious than Laslett would like to believe. Bury (1988) has undertaken a valuable review of the work of Fries (1980) on the 'rectangularization of mortality' and the 'compression of morbidity', and similarly Warnes (1993) has provided a brilliant critique of the book *Setting Limits* by Daniel Callahan (1987). Essentially Callahan, developing the implications of Fries' thesis, advocates societal acceptance that the 'natural' lifespan is roughly 80 years in length. Given this, medical treatment at older ages, he argues, should be withdrawn and resources rationed on the basis of chronological age:

> Some would say . . . age as a criterion for termination of treatment should be ruled out of bounds . . . The high cost of health care, unrelenting technological developments, and the good of the elderly themselves require that it be examined afresh.
>
> (Callahan 1987: 167–9)

It is when death (the termination of treatment) is being advocated 'for the good' of the victims themselves, that one recognizes evidence of the ultimate oppression. The phrase 'unrelenting technological developments' suggests that the debate is primarily about terminally ill (elderly) patients, in great pain and being supported to absurd lengths by hi-tech equipment. In Britain, however, the BMA has recently issued new guidelines regarding DNR (do-not-resuscitate) cases. This followed the case of an 88-year-old woman investigated by the Health Ombudsman. When she was brought into hospital with pneumonia, a DNR order was placed on her records without her being asked or her relatives consulted (*The Guardian*, 3 March 1993: 5). This form of ageism evidently operates at the level of routine health service procedure as well as in the intensive care wards. The brutality of this new form of eugenics was most clearly apparent in the words of a former Governor of Colorado: 'older people have a duty to die and get out of the way' (Friedan 1993: 510).

There has been a vigorous challenge to Callahan's arguments in the US (Barry and Bradley 1991). It is time that the prejudicial view of old age as a painful terminal condition from which people need to be released is challenged openly without qualification or reservation in Britain and elsewhere. Chronological cleansing is the ultimate act of ageism.

3

Another form of bigotry: Ageism gets on to the agenda

The previous chapter has provided ample evidence that there has always been an interest in later life and a willingness to discuss the negatives of old age and the old. Is this ageism? Before this question can be addressed, we need to study in a little more detail the concept of ageism and, again, to look at history.

Butler's initiative

Much of the research into residential care for older people in the 1960s and early 1970s was intended to expose what went on behind closed doors. Townsend (1962), Robb (1967) and Meacher (1972) are particularly well-known British examples. Although these studies do not use the word ageism, they represent well the outraged liberal sensibilities that fuelled, amongst other things, the development of the feminist and anti-racist movements of the 1960s and the early 1970s.

During the same period, gerontologists were heavily involved in debating the issues raised by disengagement theory. This postulated an inevitable mutual disengagement between the ageing person and society:

> His withdrawal may be accompanied from the outset by an increased preoccupation with himself: certain institutions may make the withdrawal easy for him.
>
> (Cumming and Henry 1961: 14)

There was an immediate response from many sociologists and gerontologists protesting that older people remain engaged and active in society (Fennell *et al.* 1988: 46–8). This concern to demonstrate the positive side of later life and, in particular, the continuing social activities of older people continued to dominate much gerontological writing during the 1970s.

Two other sociological issues of that time were the aged as a minority group

A yearning after communion

While Peter Townsend was carrying out his research for *The Last Refuge*, Jules Henry was undertaking 'a passionate ethnography' of American culture in 1962. His book, *Culture Against Man* concludes with a section on 'human obsolescence' in which he studied three hospitals: 'Taken together these three institutions give a good picture of the kinds of fates that await most of the people who become sick and obsolete in our culture.' He describes Tower Hospital as private, profit-making, comfortable and humane, contrasting with another that was profit-making but 'inhuman', and a third that was supported by public funds and was 'somewhere in between'.

> The staff, though animated by solicitude and kindliness seem to maintain an attitude of indulgent superiority to the patients whom they consider disoriented children, in need of care, but whose confusion is to be brushed off, while their bodily needs are assiduously looked after. Tower is oriented toward body and not toward mind. The mind of the patients gets in the way of the real business of the institution, which is medical care, feeding, and asepsis. Anything rational that the patient wants is given him as quickly as possible in the brisk discharge of duty, and harsh words are rare. At the same time the staff seems to have minimal understanding of the mental characteristics of an aged person. As for the patients, they live out their last days in long stretches of anxiety and silent reminiscing, punctuated by outbursts of petulance at one another, by TV viewing, and by visits from their relatives. There is no inner peace, and social life is minimal. Meanwhile the patients reach out to the researcher and would engage her endlessly in conversation if she would stay. There is a yearning after communion but no real ability to achieve it.
>
> (Henry 1965: 474)

Does this represent the kind of fate awaiting older people who become sick in the 1990s? Has anything changed?

(Barron 1953; Streib 1965) and the ageing subculture (Rose 1965). Both concepts were modelled on other debates associated with ethnic minorities and adolescence; again it is possible to see connections between these much more extensive literatures and the development of critical studies of ageing.

It was not surprising therefore that the word 'ageism' itself was introduced to represent prejudice against older people. This happened in the late 1960s as a result of the efforts of the psychiatrist, Robert Butler. Many sceptics refer to the term as having been coined by Butler, seeming to imply that it is a less than convincing concept. The critical point to appreciate is that, although Butler succeeded in putting the word on the agenda, all sorts of writers came to the subject from many different disciplines and activities, and many have subsequently made good use of Butler's initiative. As Gruman comments, through Butler ageism was 'given a history' (1978: 362).

At that time, in 1969, Butler was involved in a controversy over the proposed use of a high-rise block as public housing for the elderly located in a fashionable part of Maryland. This was covered by an article in the *Washington Post* – purportedly the first time the word 'ageism' appeared in the mass media. In the angry debates over the use of the residential block, Butler had seen the same generational conflict that had characterized the student–police battles in Chicago a year earlier. The arguments in Maryland centred upon the swimming pool, air-conditioning and parking facilities that were attached to the building. The middle-aged local residents felt they were appropriate for their boom-time home comforts, but not for the elderly, a pre-war generation that had no use or need for them. They saw the prospective old incomers as an unsettling force that threatened the peaceful harmony of their local community.

So the concept of ageism did not emerge out of academic gerontology – it originated in community action against the NIMBY tendency that still taxes us in the 1990s. It is also significant that it was a housing issue that was involved and, of course, housing policies have often reflected prejudice against other groups: the poor, women, ethnic minorities, people with disabilities and the young (Macdonald and Rich 1983: 76).

Butler and Lewis (1973) defined ageism as follows:

> Ageism can be seen as a process of systematic stereotyping of and discrimination against people because they are old, just as racism and sexism accomplish this for skin colour and gender. Old people are categorized as senile, rigid in thought and manner, old-fashioned in morality and skills . . . Ageism allows the younger generations to see older people as different from themselves, thus they subtly cease to identify with their elders as human beings.

This definition has appeared in many publications; recently, for example, in Butler's contribution to *The Encyclopedia of Aging* (Palmore 1987: 22–3). For this reason it deserves close attention and I return to it at the beginning of Chapter 9.

The response

The impact of Butler's paper was such that anti-ageism quickly became 'an enlightened prejudice' in influential circles in the US (Cole 1992: 228). Butler went on to publish a book in 1975 which elaborated his argument: *Why Survive? Being Old in America*. The word 'ageism' was included in *The American Heritage Dictionary of the English Language* for the first time in the 1979 edition. It is significant that for ten years or so there was little response from the gerontological community – what Estes has referred to as 'the aging enterprise' (Estes 1979). There was some critical discussion of stereotypes (Seltzer and Atchley 1971; Tibbits 1979) but little appeared in print that developed Butler's argument. A number of restatements of ageism were published; for example, Hendricks and Hendricks (1977) and Comfort (1977). The latter, a biologist with an international reputation based on extensive research on ageing, published a polemical book, *A Good Age*, that was directed at the coffee table market. It lauded some notable older people, and was the subject of a two-part feature in the *Sunday Times* Magazine. The first item in its encyclopaedic section reads:

> Ageism is the notion that people cease to be people, cease to be the same people or become people of a distinct and inferior kind, by virtue of having lived a specified number of years. The eighteenth-century French naturalist Georges Buffon said, 'to the philosopher, old age must be considered a prejudice.' Ageism is that prejudice.
>
> (Comfort 1977: 35)

Comfort's literary style, much bolder than Butler's, together with the forceful marketing of this book, helped to establish ageism in the popular consciousness.

New ageism

The first published challenge to Butler came from Kalish in 1979. He argued that there was a 'new ageism' typified by the claims:

> that 'we' understand how badly you are being treated, that 'we' have the tools to improve your treatment, and that if you adhere to our program, 'we' will make your life considerably better. You are poor, lonely, weak, incompetent, ineffectual, and no longer terribly bright. You are sick, in need of better housing and transportation and nutrition, and we – the nonelderly and those elderly who align themselves with us and work with us – are finally going to turn our attention to you, the deserving elderly, and relieve you from ageism.
>
> (Kalish 1979: 398)

Kalish argued that the first part of Butler's book, focusing on this Incompetent Failure Model, may have had more impact than the later part which focused on a better way of life for older people, and that the effect of this may have been to promote and reinforce this 'new ageism'. This argument was taken up more aggressively by Cole (1986), but first Levin and Levin, two sociologists who had studied racism, entered the fray. In the preface to their book they make the following telling comment:

> The literature of gerontology has consistently reported and emphasized decline, whether physical, psychological, or social, in the characteristics and capacities of the aged.
>
> (Levin and Levin 1980: ix)

Their focus is primarily upon the concept of decline: for them ageism is equivalent to the assumption of inevitable decline. Coming from outside they saw the ageing enterprise, and gerontology in particular, as having contributed significantly to the knowledge base of ageism through the collection and documentation of evidence that substantiates the assumption of decline.

Butler's definition received further critical attention from Schonfield (1982). In the title of his article, Schonfield posed the challenging question: 'Who is stereotyping whom and why?' He begins his discussion with a definition of ageism based solely upon prejudicial attitudes. He then asserts:

An unbiased observer of everyday encounters in western societies would surely not find a preponderance of unkindness by people under 65 toward people over 65.

(Schonfield 1982: 270)

He accuses Butler of confusing attitudes towards one's own ageing with attitudes toward older people:

Holding negative attitudes toward older people merely because they are old is immoral, according to well-nigh universally accepted ethical standards. But is there anything immoral about disliking some of the concomitants of ageing processes?

(Schonfield 1982: 271)

Schonfield goes on to quote three eminent gerontologists who, he suggests, have hinted that commentators (by implication, including Butler) have misinterpreted research data. For example, he quotes Ethel Shanas: 'Why [do] we Americans who are interacting with our older relatives in a helping way persist in believing that we are neglecting our elderly?' (Shanas 1979: 9). Schonfield concludes his attack upon anti-ageists with the comment:

The mixture of altruism and egoism has caused them to misread the evidence. When the prevalence of ageism is said to be supported by avowed feelings of greater loss on the death of an 18-year-old than on the death of a 75-year-old, it is time to stop or at least to think again.

(Schonfield 1982: 272)

In Schonfield's view contemporary society does not hold negative attitudes towards older people; younger people, by and large, act in a kind and helpful manner towards their seniors; disliking some of the consequences of age is not morally reprehensible; regretting the deaths of younger people more than those of older people is not improper; and anti-ageists such as Butler are guilty of stereotyping society.

Cole mounted a rather different critique drawing upon his historical study of ageing, particularly that of nineteenth-century Christian America. He argued that:

Ageism and its critics represent the alternating, dominant voices of an American fugue on the theme of growing old – a fugue in which successive singers have performed variations of the same part, since the early nineteenth century.

(Cole 1992: 228)

The message Cole sought to convey was that current concerns with promoting a positive view of ageing and with attacking negative stereotypes are just part of the ongoing dualism or ambivalence with which old age has always been perceived.

In 1980, Butler published an elaboration of his argument which helped to move discussion away from personal attitudes. He distinguished between prejudicial attitudes, discriminatory practices and institutional policies:

> All three have contributed to the transformation of aging from a natural process into a social problem in which the elderly individual bears the detrimental consequences.
>
> (Butler 1980: 8)

It would have been easy for Butler to have attacked the myths and stereotypes that underpin the attitudes of the public towards old people, and to use the parallels with sexism and racism to blame discrimination upon individual prejudice. His notable achievement, over and above that of launching the concept of ageism, was to link the individual and the institutional aspects in one definition: in this respect the words *systematic* and *categorized* are critical components of his definition.

de Beauvoir

Around the same time that Butler was publishing his critique of ageist America, Simone de Beauvoir was working on her book *La Vieillesse* which was published in France in 1970. Woodward (1988: 28) describes it as 'a prodigious effort to explore the roots of ageism from social, economic and psychological perspectives'.

By and large, the book has been poorly received. Upon being published in the US, 'it met with a wave of censure by journalists and gerontologists alike for its dark and tragic portrait of old age' (Woodward 1988: 28). Stearns, for example, describes her approach as that of 'the usually bitter old literati' (1977: 12). Butler was particularly critical:

> [Her book] was motivated by her desire to improve the treatment of the elderly in Western civilization. Ironically, her book's purpose was offset by her reinforcement of a multitude of stereotypes about aging . . . Her work suffers from incomplete scholarship, ideology, elitism, and obvious subjectivity as regards aging. It is probable that de Beauvoir worked from the armchair in Parisian libraries and made few forays among the elderly. She detests aging and the older person in herself.
>
> (Butler 1978: 389)

Fischer was exceptional in referring to it as 'a learned, graceful and intelligent work' (1978: 20). Finley (1984) is ambivalent: 'brilliant though flawed . . . the only synoptic work of its kind that I know'. More recently, Greer has commented, 'de Beauvoir does not show any signs of realization that her view of old age was wildly distorted' (1991: 280).

What is regrettable, however, is not de Beauvoir's delusions but rather that there should have been such a censorious response to a book that was intended: 'to break the conspiracy of silence . . . I call upon my readers to help me in doing so' (de Beauvoir 1977: 8, 14).

The main body of the book is divided into two sections: 'Old Age Seen from Without' and 'The Being-in-the-World':

> In the first part of this book . . . I shall examine what biology, anthropology, history and contemporary sociology have to tell us about old age.

In the second I shall do my best to describe the way in which the aged man inwardly apprehends his relationship with his body, with time and with the outside world.

(de Beauvoir 1977: 16)

The distinction between these two contrasting approaches is crucial to understanding her critique. Whereas Butler approached ageism as an established and successful middle-aged psychiatrist, someone who had a command of contemporary gerontological knowledge and who was eager to challenge societal assumptions about old people, de Beauvoir based her book on her own experience of approaching old age after a long career as an influential French intellectual and partner of Jean-Paul Sartre. As for so many other successful people (as implied by Stearns), this had been something of a revelatory and demoralizing experience:

What a furious outcry I raised when I offended against this taboo [against talk of old age] at the end of *La Force des Choses*! Acknowledging that I was on the threshold of old age was tantamount to saying that old age was lying there in wait for every woman, and that it had already laid hold upon many of them. Great numbers of people, particularly old people, told me kindly or angrily but always at great length and again and again, that old age simply did not exist!

(de Beauvoir 1977: 7)

What both Butler and de Beauvoir share is this assumption that old age, and thereby old people, indisputably exist. They diverge only in Butler's inclination to adopt a positive view and de Beauvoir's much more pessimistic approach. Also, like Butler and Comfort, de Beauvoir raises one critical element of ageism (one that many older people articulate): that old people are seen as sub- or non-human. Whereas Butler points to younger generations for whom older people 'subtly cease' to be human beings, de Beauvoir comments:

When their economic status is decided upon, society appears to think that they belong to an entirely different species: for if all that is needed to feel that one has done one's duty by them is to grant them a wretched pittance, then they have neither the same needs nor the same feelings as other men.

(de Beauvoir 1977: 9)

Like Comfort, de Beauvoir made a remarkable contribution to the establishment of a popular anti-ageist consciousness. Both, for example, were quoted by Gladys Elder in her book *The Alienated* (1977). One cannot overestimate the significance of someone of de Beauvoir's standing in the intellectual world joining in the study of the experience of ageing. At the same time there is little disputing that her commentary on her research was greatly affected by her own feelings about age as she approached what she perceived to be her own old age. The critical point about 'the literati' is that the famous and successful do approach later life from a distinctive angle. As Minois comments:

Simone de Beauvoir has already drawn attention to the fact that the witness of literary men should often be treated cautiously: 'Law-givers and poets always belong to the privileged classes, which is one of the reasons why their words have no great value. They never say anything but part truths and very often they lie.' This statement is, however, dangerous and excessive and could too easily rebound on its author, as a bourgeois renegade branded by her class origins.

(Minois 1989: 48)

The famous have achieved a certain success that has been publicly acclaimed. Many view their approaching old age with alarm. They fear a decline in their reputation and, as they witness and sometimes participate in the humiliations of their seniors (for example, in television programmes such as 'This Is Your Life'), they may begin to declaim in public the miseries that they have come to associate with age.

The elderly mystique

In 1965, Rosalie Rosenfelt published the following astute account of the *Elderly Mystique* modelled on Betty Friedan's famous 1963 work *The Feminine Mystique*.

> We know that many a person at some point late in life comes to consider himself old, and this implies he views himself as different in important respects from what he considered himself to have been earlier. According to the mystique, this point marks an unmitigated misfortune, which a series of lugubrious losses, deficits and declines has forced upon his attention. Despite his grim determination to 'think young' destiny has had the last laugh and has forced him to the mat for the final countdown . . .
>
> While the old person is taking stock of himself, he might as well become resigned to being 'behind the times', for it is inconceivable he should have kept abreast of them. As a worker, he has become a liability. His rigidity, his out-of-date training, his proneness to disabling illness, not to mention his irritability, lowered efficiency and arrogant manner, all militate against the likelihood of his being hired or promoted . . .
>
> The nadir of the process is, of course, institutionalization of the aged – not always a necessary or desirable outcome, to be sure, but a practical method of storage until death. Providing the old one learns to conform to the inmate culture, this solution by storage should not be too difficult, although it is recognized he might have preferred another fate – slow torture.

(Rosenfelt 1965: 37–43)

What this demonstrates is how, in the 1960s, the standard gerontological model of later life was the older male industrial worker. The implication of Rosenfelt's argument, like that of Friedan's, is that this negative scenario is a self-fulfilling prophecy.

Feminism and ageism

Following de Beauvoir, feminists such as Sontag (1978), Macdonald and Rich (1983), Itzin (1984, 1986), Walker (1985), Greer (1991) and Friedan (1993) have made important contributions in clarifying the complex relationship between ageism and sexism. Arber and Ginn (1991) have produced a review of the evidence of how older women suffer from the consequences of both ageism and sexism. They provide a concise argument of how a patriarchal society exercises power through the chronologies of employment and reproduction, and through the sexualized promotion of a youthful appearance in women. There can be little doubting the double jeopardy thesis that older women suffer doubly (at least) as a result of both forms of prejudice (Chappell and Havens 1980; Itzin 1984). Women have been at the forefront of a number of anti-ageist initiatives mounted by older people, most well-known perhaps being Maggie Kuhn of the Gray Panthers.

What is interesting (certainly for an outsider to observe) is the problems that women in the post-1960s feminist movement have had in coming to recognize the significance of age (Macdonald and Rich 1983; Rosenthal 1990). It seems that as the 60s generation has come face to face with ageism, so another – younger – generation is acquiring power within the movement, a generation that is equipped with the much-respected energy and passion of youth. This kind of generational dynamic affects many groups that are committed to promoting age-related change, not least those within the pensioners' movement. There is always a feeling of disillusion among the older members as younger ones discover and take command of the wheel.

The contribution of older people

Laslett begins his book with the following statement:

> This book on ageing, and on ageing in Britain particularly, belongs wholly to the later life of its author. My first writing on the history of ageing, and the earliest treatment of that subject, appeared when I was sixty-one and nearly all the rest of the work was done in my later sixties and earlier seventies. Here then is a report on experience as well as an exploratory analysis. It is in itself a project of an individual Third Age.
>
> (Laslett 1989: vi)

It is interesting to contrast Laslett's statement with that of de Beauvoir (page 34). She was writing in anticipation of old age, from a position of expectation of what she perceived to be its threshold. Her priority was to break the silence on the reality of the old age in prospect, and she might have agreed with Laslett that it was a project of her third age, but one based on anticipatory research not experience. Other people who have been successful and famous in other fields have similarly taken up the challenge of age at the point of perceiving them- selves as having reached a certain threshold in life – Jack Jones, for example, has been at the forefront of the pensioners movement in Britain since retiring from his position as General Secretary of the Transport and General Workers Union in 1977. What is significant about de Beauvoir and Laslett is that they each drew upon their scholarly skills rather than on the experiences of their contemporaries. The alternative, the traditional ethnographic approach, is to interview, listen to, and study the lives of an appropriate sample of older people.

Ethnography

Consider the introduction of Ford and Sinclair:

> We set out to uncover and report upon the lives of older women, concentrating upon a more complete account of their thoughts, feelings and activities. We became interested in the lives of older women because we were involved in visiting them, either as part of volunteer schemes or as neighbours and friends . . . We wanted to obtain personal accounts of the lives of a group of women, presenting them in the women's own words.
>
> (Ford and Sinclair 1987: 5)

Many other researchers have approached older people in a similar way, seeking to 'give voice to their feelings', to produce accounts of their lives in their own words. Often this is done with tape-recorders and with the interviewee being photographed, so that the reader does gain a very real sense of hearing older people talk. Nevertheless, we should never underestimate the power of the authors or editors to determine which voices and which words the reader hears. Who did the older women interviewed by Ford and Sinclair represent? What kinds of older women become involved in volunteer schemes, become known to their neighbours or develop friendships and so enter the networks of the two researchers? Who refused or were unable to participate? To ask these kinds of critical questions is not to question the value of Ford and Sinclair's book for the study of ageism. It includes, for example, the testimony of Mrs Hatter. We could not hope for any more powerful testimony of the oppressive quality of ageism:

> I'll tell you what happened with my pension book. They have it here, they take it when you come in to help keep you and they give you so much back as spending money. I think they decide how much you get. In fact I do not know how much the pension is now. I've told them that they are to let me know when it's due again. It's nice to know. I know it belongs to me, but they have it. You never see the book. They never say anything about it.
>
> (Ford and Sinclair 1987: 36)

Without doubting for one moment the authenticity of Mrs Hatter's statement, the difficult question still has to be addressed: what does it represent? Is her experience typical or eccentric?

Between these two extremes of library research by older people and field-work by younger researchers, there are two important ways in which older people have contributed to our understanding of later life, and ageism in particular. One is through personal research into the lives and circumstances of contemporaries and a particularly significant example of this is Elder (1977). The second is personal testimony published in person, not through an intermediary.

Becoming angry

The following is the Preface from Gladys Elder's book *The Alienated: Growing Old Today*:

I began to talk to all the elderly around me. I tried to cultivate insight, understanding and patience, and as I pondered on the life stories I pieced together I became angry. I watched my acquaintances shopping, I had no difficulty in seeing the economic limitations, the scraping and stinting to which so many are condemned. Sometimes I sat at home, reflecting, thinking back over the years, seeing those lives against a familiar background – my own. I thought of the devastating times my elderly neighbours had lived through, of their deprivations so stoically borne – and my anger increased. Anger is a fine spur and very soon I had gathered together enough material to start along the hard road of authorship. For, growing with the anger, I had a vision. A vision of comfort, peace and rest for the elderly, achieved not by charity and well-meant aid from the outside, but by the concerted actions within this group, in other words, *by themselves* . . . At 75, I know very well what aging is, what it feels like after a lifetime's struggle, to find oneself among society's cast-offs, duly labelled and slotted into the compartment called OAP . . .

Books on old age by sociologists, psychologists and gerontologists are growing in number, a hopeful sign that the subject is at least receiving due attention. *Yet none has been written by an OAP*; this distinction makes me feel I am well-placed to plead this case.

(Elder 1977: 13–15)

Personal testimony

As with the literary work of prisoners, personal testimony is often produced in the most difficult of situations. A famous example is Ellen Newton's diary.

Incidents and conversations are set down exactly as they happened, sometimes while they were actually happening. Gaps here and there, sometimes of days, sometimes of months, are due to illness, intrusive curiosity as to what I was writing about, and some editing at a later stage to improve the narrative. Very often I wrote in the small hours, and in the morning, in pencil, mostly, on salvaged spare pages of notebooks and the backs of used envelopes. These bits and pieces were scattered in bags and boxes for want of a desk to hold them.

(Newton 1980: 1)

In 1983 May Sarton published a novel centred on the experience of Caro, a person in a similar position to Ellen Newton:

I am not mad, only old. I make this statement to give me courage. To give you an idea what I mean by courage, suffice it to say that it has taken two weeks for me to obtain this notebook and a pen. I am in a concentration

'I watched my acquaintances shopping, I had no difficulty in seeing the economic limitations, the scraping and stinting to which so many are condemned' (Elder 1977: 13–15)
Photograph: Brenda Price, Format

camp for the old, a place where people dump their parents or relatives exactly as though it were an ash can.

(Sarton 1983: 9)

In 1990 Sarton herself kept a diary for one whole year in which she documented her growing problems with chronic illness:

Should I publish this journal at all? What value does it have, coming from a diminished old Sarton? I hope I am right in thinking that flawed though it is, it does have value, if only in suggesting how one old lady has dealt over a year with chronic pain; what the rewards are of living here by the sea, even old and ill; how I have had to learn to be dependent.

(Sarton 1993: 10)

These are examples of the literary work of older people who have sought to document the realities of later life, both subjective and objective. Very different strategies have been adopted. Each has strengths and weaknesses. It is when they are studied together that the evidence regarding ageism becomes indisputable.

Direct action

There are many other areas of activity in which the same goals have been pursued. It is, of course, difficult to present a comprehensive account of this since so much goes unrecorded – action in local public meetings, representations to the authorities, the debates in voluntary organizations and self-help groups, the raising of funds and the resulting arguments on the doorstep and in the high street, the petitions and the mass lobbies of parliament, and so on.

One of the most difficult forms of individual action is appearing in a television documentary. Towards the end of 1993, there were two television programmes, broadcast on successive nights, which provided two contrasting examples. First there was a film of the meeting of four young male neo-nazis with three survivors of Auschwitz. Although more a confrontation of generations and cultures, the viewer could not but be impressed by the courage of the survivors who, each in turn, faced the four bigoted men in locations associated with their own vivid memories of past atrocities. Outnumbered, there was a sense of humiliation as they each appeared to fail in getting the young men to hear what they had to say and to accept the evidence of genocide.

The following night, three pensioners were shown travelling from Bridlington to Blackpool. They planned to confront the Chancellor of the Exchequer at the 1992 Tory Party Conference, over his proposal to impose Value Added Tax on domestic fuel. They were not experienced campaigners and once again the viewer witnessed older people being publicly humiliated. They sought and failed to get a powerful younger person to hear what they had to say. He did not recognize that people might die as a direct result of the proposed increased taxation.

It has often been argued that the only effective political action is organized collective campaigning. Commentators often point to the potential voting power of the elderly, but politicians by and large have not responded to the threat. The historical record is depressing. In the UK, there has been an enormous investment by older people in the various pensioner organizations but their efforts have often been wasted by internal conflict and political timidity (Blaikie 1990). In 1983, for example, Margaret Thatcher visited Swansea. A broad alliance of local organizations and unions collaborated in an enormous and largely peaceful march through the city centre. For those of us who took part it was an exhilarating and novel experience marching with so many friends and colleagues down the Kingsway. The joint committee of the pensioners' organizations, however, fearful of trouble, were taking part at the same time in a rally they had organized in a chapel hall in Morriston. Mrs Thatcher had been invited but she was, of course, otherwise engaged, scurrying past the mass demonstration on Oystermouth Road.

The Gray Panthers

Over the last twenty years the Gray Panthers have often been seen to be the model for collective political action by older people in the future. This movement was launched in 1970 by Maggie Kuhn and five other involuntary retirees to protest about the Vietnam War. Its association with revolutionary anarchic action is evident in an early press statement:

We did not select our name; the name selected us. It describes who we are: 1) we are older persons in retirement; 2) we are aware of the revolutionary nature of our time; 3) although we differ with the strategy and tactics of some militant groups in our society we share with them many of the goals of human freedom, dignity and self development; and 4) we have a sense of humour.

(Butler 1975: 340–1)

Kuhn was particularly concerned about the patronage implicit in the word 'play'. She described Golden Age Clubs as glorified playpens. During the 1970s they campaigned on race (organizing a Black House Conference on Aging), health (paying a 'house call' on a Convention of the American Medical Association), television (getting the Code of Ethics to include references to age), the hearing aid industry and nursing home abuse (Phillipson 1982: 135; Friedan 1993: 609–12). Gerontological research was not overlooked either. Estes quotes a pamphlet distributed by the Gray Panthers at the annual meeting of the Gerontological Society in San Francisco in 1977:

Gerontology has assumed the deterioration of the aged, and has attempted to describe it in terms which ignore the social and economic factors which in large measure precipitate that deterioration. By reifying the attribute 'old', gerontology reinforces societal attitudes which view older people as stuck in an inevitable chronological destiny of decay and deterioration.

(Estes 1979: 226)

By the end of the 1970s the Gray Panthers had a membership of 15,000 throughout the United States. Friedan (1993: 610) provides an up-to-date account of current activities: a national health plan, affordable housing, flexible work and retirement schedules, and increased intergenerational networking.

In conclusion, the history of ageism as a political idea, a phenomenon which challenges the beliefs and reasoning of individuals and institutions, is only twenty-something years old. Older people have always been aware of the prejudice and discrimination they have suffered, but only since the cultural revolution of the 1960s has there been any kind of recognition of this among younger people. It is clear that the biggest challenge is that posed by Kalish's 'new ageists': people who know they should be against ageism and purport to be so, but who patronize older people, making decisions for them, telling funny stories about them, and feeling good that they are looking after them.

PART II

Aspects of ageism

In the previous two chapters, I have viewed the historical backdrop to the ageism of the mid-1990s. What I have tried to demonstrate is how both old age and ageism are no more than ideas, ways of thinking – but that, as such, they reflect enormously powerful cultural forces. In many societies the idea of old age has been a critical element in structuring both the life course and the population: structuring in the sense of making distinctions and imposing roles and expectations upon individuals within the created categories. In contrast, ageism is a new construct, as yet poorly understood, but part of a broader movement that disputes these structuring distinctions and the ways in which social inequalities are preserved and the individual's freedoms constrained.

In the next four chapters, the second part of the book, I focus on various aspects of modern society and of life in the late twentieth century: areas in which ageism appears to have some significant impact. The health and social services frequently set the agenda for discussions about the elderly and it is probably true that most practitioners and service providers who specialize in the elderly are employed in this area. Nevertheless ageism extends into all parts of modern society. For this reason I decided to ignore the service-oriented classification of topics – health, income, housing, social welfare, and so on – and to adopt a rather more sociological set of themes: power, language, interpersonal relations and organization.

It is not possible to provide a full consideration of each issue covered – my priority is to provide some empirical evidence and to raise some of the relevant questions. Only in Part III will I begin to draw some of the strings together.

4

The government of old men: Ageism and power

Sociologists have long recognized the problems of defining power. Giddens (1979: 69) points out the distinction between power defined as the capability of individual actors to achieve their will and as a property of institutions and collectivities. Closely linked to this is the contrast between the exercise of power through action and the fundamental aspect of power in a social structure. These contrasts reflect the distinction between the ageism of individuals and that of organizations and society. It is one thing for the malevolent individual to abuse an older relative; another for the National Health Service to institute procedures that deny people over a certain age treatments and services they need. In both cases, however, older people suffer.

It is easy to think of older people suffering as a result of the power of ageism, but this would be to confuse ideology (ageism) with the holder of power (individual or organization) and to presume that the individual wielders of power are younger people. Thinking of power as being integral to social structure corresponds to the idea that human society is intrinsically ageist – individual agents do not need to act in offensive ways or to be a certain age in order that the institutions they represent be ageist.

When we think about old age and old people, particularly if we are involved in the provision of services to those in need, we are inclined to think of them as poor, deprived and powerless. Currently in the 1990s there is much talk about empowerment (Parsloe and Stevenson 1993). Implicit in this is the idea that those in need are powerless. However, those with the power in these situations are of an age themselves – councillors, directors, committee members, etc. – and often it is said that they are 'too old': that what is needed are younger people with energy, vision and experience of modern-day methods. So ageism is also involved in the ways in which people endeavour to gain, retain and exercise power.

This argument suggests that it may be more profitable to focus upon the relationship between age and power than between age and deprivation, even though, of course, the two are closely connected.

Gerontocracies

In ancient Greece, power came with age. Plato proposed that 'it is for elder men to rule and for younger to submit' (1975: 178). And, using a very similar formula, Thomas asserts that 'in early modern England the prevailing ideal was gerontocratic: the young were to serve and the old were to rule' (1977: 207).

Over the years we have seen how successful politicians such as Churchill, Mitterand, Mao Tse-Tung and Reagan have been able to maintain political power through their skills in managing political processes. Theirs reflect many comparable histories in the diverse and less famous worlds of local politics, business life and families. Typically, however, a time comes, usually in anticipation of death, when even the most successful and powerful have to stand down and their power passes on to others. In prior anticipation of this there are times when older politicians are widely perceived to be holding on to power well beyond what is reasonable. On television we have witnessed the pitiful images of Brezhnev and Hastings Banda, seriously ill and handicapped people struggling to retain their political power to the very end. Sometimes such leaders are of a generation that played a major part in revolutionizing the state and who now are being succeeded − begrudgingly − by a younger generation. Sometimes the older generation appears to be concerned primarily with celebrating past achievements and conserving traditional structures.

It is easy to see in these situations the unavoidable realities of finitude: the observation that no one can live for ever is a universal cliché. We all have to give way at some point. Judging the point at which someone should give up power, however, depends upon all kinds of contentious considerations. Essentially what is in question is trust, competence and capability, but these are three intangibles that are open to political debate. What is more easily assessed is age. It is the ways in which age is popularly associated with these other concepts that reveals much of the ageism that undermines even the most powerful, respected or beloved of politicians.

At the point of succession, the retiring power-holder may attempt to dictate who succeeds. Frequently this last exercise in power appears to be based upon affection and obligation as much as sound judgement, typically involving two kinds of relations: filial descendants and long-time friends and compatriots. An excess of inheritance by descendants leads to accusations of a political dynasty. When it is old friends who succeed, then the political system is perceived to be a gerontocracy.

Nineteenth-century France

Eisele (1979) has argued that the study of the concept of gerontocracy provides interesting insights into age prejudice. He credits a Frenchman, Jean-Jacques Fazy, with inventing the term in 1828. The title of the pamphlet produced by Fazy is translated as: 'On gerontocracy, or the abuse of the wisdom of old men in the government of France'. Eisele reviewed Fazy's argument somewhat sceptically: 'a short-circuiting leap in logic . . . the essence of prejudicial thinking' (1979: 405). What Fazy does in one bald statement is confirm that the concept of gerontocracy is indeed relevant to the study of ageism:

> Gerontocracy, or the government of old men, is, according to me, the cause of all the difficulties that we see in the soul of the country.
>
> (Fazy, quoted by Eisele 1979: 404)

In France at that time, eligibility to vote began at age 30. The age at which one could stand as a deputy was raised around the time of Fazy's pamphlet from 30 to 40 years. There were many constraints on participation in the political institutions such as a sizable income requirement for candidates, but Fazy latched on to age: the legislative body was, in his opinion, of 'advanced age' and the soul of France was threatened.

Twentieth-century China

In elaborating the concept of gerontocracy, Eisele makes reference to discussions of recent governments in the US, the Soviet Union and China. Were these gerontocracies? Was government by old men the cause of all their difficulties? We all have vivid memories of the crisis in Beijing in the summer of 1989. It seemed that the familiar intergenerational conflict between students and government was to be fought out on an unprecedented scale in the capital city of the largest nation in the world. In the week before the battle of Tiananmen Square, *The Guardian* published the following account of moves in the leadership of the Chinese government:

DENG RUMOUR SPARKS JOB STRUGGLE

Rumours that Mr Deng Xiaoping is in poor health are being taken seriously by diplomats in Beijing and some believe his contemporaries have now joined the succession struggle. Mr Deng has not been seen or heard of since he met the Soviet leader, Mr Mikhail Gorbachev, a fortnight ago. Soviet sources said that he appeared to have been drugged before the meeting and had difficulty focusing his thoughts. Chinese sources claim that Mr Deng has already suffered from two minor strokes and has been in hospital recently. Several sources alleged that he relies on an oxygen mask. Rumours that Mr Deng is at death's door are a perennial feature of Beijing, but he will be 85 in August and some Western diplomats believe the question of his health is now influencing the current power struggle. The political struggle has undermined Mr Deng's standing and at the same time a number of octogenarian veterans have taken a prominent role. 'The party elders are now demanding a greater share of political power and are vying to succeed him,' a Western diplomat said. Among the candidates are President Yang Shangkun, aged 82, who is in robust health and announced the martial law declaration on May 19. Another is his predecessor, Mr Li Xiannian, aged 80, a hardliner who made a veiled criticism of Mr Deng in his speech in favour of martial law last weekend. The influential but rarely seen Mr Chun Yun, the 83-year-old economist who is thought to have clashed with Mr Deng over the pace and scope of the

economic reforms, joins the list. The most openly critical veteran is Mr
Peng Zhen, aged 86, who was Mr Deng's deputy and mayor of Beijing until
Mr Deng betrayed him at the start of the Cultural Revolution in order to
protect himself.

(*The Guardian*, 1 June 1989: 10)

Three years later, changes began to take place:

BEIJING'S OLD GUARD RESIGNS IN SHAKE-UP

In the most far-reaching reshuffle in the Chinese leadership since the
Beijing massacre of 1989, eight members of the ruling politburo have
asked to step down . . . The eight, representing more than half of the old
politburo, include the Chinese president, Yang Shangkun, aged 85; the
defence minister, Qin Jiwei; and the leader of the parliament, Wan Li, who
are all believed to be supporters of the reform campaign of China's elder
statesman, Deng Xiaoping. Three noted hardliners, Yao Yilin, Song Pin and
Li Ximing, will also go. The newspaper did not give reasons for these
retirements, but with all of those involved aged over 65, and the
Communist Party committed to replacing the old with the young, age was
clearly a factor. The departures leave what is known as the 'third
generation' of the Chinese leadership finally in place, though with dozens
of octogenarians and septuagenarians lurking in the half-light behind the
official power structure, it would be premature to conclude that the third
generation is now in power. The drive to develop a young and reformist
leadership at every level of the party has been one of the main themes of
the week-long congress, and those who fill the newly vacant places in the
politburo are likely to be outright supporters of reform and of Mr Deng.
Another trend expected to emerge from this weekend's voting for the
party central committee is promotion for the 'princelings' – the power-
hungry offspring of the top leadership. Mr Deng, aged 86, relies increasingly on a clutch of able and ambitious daughters to carry out his will. One
of them, Deng Nan, is already a government minister and is expected to
advance to the central committee. Mr Deng's greatest political enemy,
Chen Yun, aged 90, also has powerful offspring in the person of Chen
Yuan, vice-governor of the central bank. Chen junior, however, is less
loyal than the younger Dengs, brazenly announcing to the media this
week that his father was 'old and sick and out of touch'. Most party and
government elders, have likewise now deployed a network of junior
relatives in key positions and conversely there are few top rank leaders of
the third generation who do not have influential family behind them.

(*The Guardian*, 17 October 1992)

These two long accounts provide clear evidence of the importance of age, and
in particular of its association with health, in on-going struggles over political
power. It is possible that Deng's survival of the crisis of 1989 led to a switch
away from his contemporaries towards his descendants. The concept of
generation is also shown to be particularly important in a country that still has
a generation of political leaders who have personal memories of revolution.
Incidentally, it is interesting to note that Deng is reported to have celebrated his

85th birthday in August 1990 and to be only 86 in October 1992. Even on the facts of age nothing is certain.

Political generations acquire an identity through a group of leaders sharing certain critical historical experiences. In time the survivors often develop a degree of entrenchment and mutual support which, despite a continuing commitment to the same political goals, conflicts with the aspirations and priorities of members of a younger generation. It seems that the critical elements in this situation are shared experience and informal intra-generational solidarity – a matter of generation not age. This, it would appear, is what characterizes modern China but not nineteenth-century France and, on this basis, it could be argued that it was the latter that was the more ageist society. Ageism in the context of modern China is most apparent in the ways in which western diplomats and political commentators associate the failings of the leadership with their age.

The 54-year-old boy wonder

The following commentary is overtly about the inter-generation power struggle in Japan in 1991. Like the reports on China it also reveals much about age, generations and gerontocracies:

> Mr Hashimoto has all the time in the world. At 54, he is something of a boy wonder in the gerontocratic world of the LDP. The Finance Minister's youth is one of his main problems. He was pipped at the post by Mr Kaifu in a leadership tussle two years ago this week partly because he was considered much too young – his elevation to the premiership would have ushered in a new generation of conservative politicians, dashing the hopes of party leaders such as Kilchi Miyazawa, aged 71, and Michio Watanabe, aged 68, who still see themselves as prime ministerial candidates. Mr Hashimoto was also judged too independent, too sure of himself and too clever.
>
> (*The Guardian*, 7 August 1991: 9)

This example succinctly illustrates the connections between age, power, the historical process and the identification of political generations. However, the terminology includes a certain ageist sarcasm ('boy wonder') that fails to recognize the inconsistency between the notion that the LDP is a gerontocratic world and the prospects of a new generation being ushered in. There is a failure to recognize the difference between the ebb and flow of political generations and the institution of regulations and procedures which ensure that younger people are excluded from full participation.

The legal world

Magistrates and juries

It is well known that there is discrimination against older people in the labour market (page 102). Apart from the impact that this has on income, it restricts our choices on how we occupy our time. It is less well known that there are similar age bars on the appointment of magistrates. Such voluntary work is a sector of activity in which older people are frequently urged to participate.

> We looked forward to applying to become magistrates when we retired at the age of 60, as we felt we had something to offer, and would at last have the spare time required.
>
> When the time came we discovered to our dismay that the latest age at which one can become a magistrate is 55 – beyond that age it is considered that, as the initial training takes three years, and the retirement age for magistrates is 70, it is a waste of money training older people.
>
> Imagine our surprise, then, when we read recently that there is a shortage of magistrates! It's a funny old world, isn't it?
>
> (*The Guardian*, 14 July 1992: 20)

Age bars are often defended on the grounds that it would be invidious to assess individual competence, and that an age limit is non-discriminatory. Although it could be embarrassing if competence were to be assessed, a certain proven ability to assess evidence and formulate sound judgements is critical if magistrates are to have the confidence of the public. An age limit is 'non-discriminatory' only insofar as it does not discriminate on grounds other than age: it is unambiguously discriminatory not to consider one applicant aged 55 while giving careful attention to another aged 54, and it is absurd to lose competent and experienced magistrates simply because they reach the age of 70.

When organizations decide upon their policies regarding the holding of office, there is often a tendency to confuse age with length of service. It is sometimes feared that people will cling to office too long or that over the years a clique, a gerontocracy, will come to dominate. But this is no argument for using age as the basis for terminating office and not length of service. So the alternative procedure would be the fixed term of service, say ten years, which is renewable subject to the magistrate re-applying.

The appointment of people to serve on a jury is another example of an age bar. Until recently the ancient right of jury service was denied to those over 65. In 1988, however, this was extended to 70. This was seen by those who lobbied for the reform as a step towards the complete removal of the age bar. For others it was a way of increasing the number of citizens able and willing to serve – without impinging upon the time of the 'economically active'. What is interesting is that many older people objected to this reform and protested to those who advocated it (Midwinter 1990: 50). They claimed that older people are less able to see, hear and concentrate: in fact all manner of disabilities were identified. They felt that age, and indeed all of these incapacities, should *automatically* disqualify one from jury service. The alternative view is that people over 70 should complain vociferously about not being allowed to serve. They should recognize that, as things stand, in the event of their being charged with offences under the law, the verdict will be passed by a jury exclusively made up of younger people.

Judges

Many people have deplored the great age of judges: 'They're too old for the job! They ought to be made to retire like the rest of us!' There is a resentment of the gerontocratic world of the courts: too much power rests in the hands of people who are too out-of-touch, too old-fashioned and too old. A survey undertaken by the *Solicitors Journal* in 1992 found that 65 per cent of the British public agree with the statement: 'Judges are out of touch with ordinary people and everyday life', and 86 per cent thought that judges should retire earlier (*The Observer Magazine*, 13 December 1992: 32–9). Consider, however, what lies behind the following comment that appeared in a newspaper profile of Lord Scarman:

> As a populist he has burst out of the clichéd straitjacket of the male, old, remote and out-of-touch judge. Male he is, old he may be. But he is neither remote nor wholly out of touch . . . As a practising lawyer he was as conservative as any in his casework. The reforming urge came to him late in life, at an age when most people are contemplating putting their feet up in a rose-strewn cottage in the countryside. He was 63 when he first proposed a bill of rights, 70 when he conducted the Brixton inquiry and 75 when he adopted the civil rights campaigns.
>
> (*The Guardian*, 29 July 1991: 17)

What might have been the consequences of forcing Lord Scarman to retire at 65? More to the point, reviewing what he has accomplished in his pensionable years, we should regret what society has lost by dispatching millions of talented people to their equivalent of a rose-strewn cottage. The problem of incompetent judges is not solved by imposing the automatic age bar that has denuded so many other sectors of society of talent and experience.

Fear

There are many members of Lord Scarman's generation who feel threatened by crime and unprotected by the forces of law and order. The popular perception of increased risks from crime in older age, however, is inaccurate. The British Crime Survey (Mayhew *et al.* 1988) shows that people aged 16 to 30 are over four times more at risk of crime than those over 60. Yet a quarter of people over 60 gave mugging as the reason why they felt unsafe when out at night.

As we age, we may feel increasingly vulnerable and our fear of external threats may grow. We may suspect that power is passing into the hands of dangerous young gangs, and that the police are losing control of the streets and public places. The tendency then is to hide and to withdraw behind locked doors. When frightened of crime, many of us will impose a curfew on

Poll tax defaulters

Often the age of older people who break the law is perceived to be an explanation, and an excuse, for their behaviour. The following is taken from a newspaper story. Names have been fictionalized.

A council behaved unlawfully and unreasonably in trying to send two disabled pensioners to prison for allegedly not paying their poll tax, a High Court judge ruled yesterday.

George Smith, aged 74, is an acute epileptic and Doris Smith, aged 80, is wheelchair-bound and incontinent. They have both suffered psychiatric damage in the course of their 18-month legal battle with the council.

Mr Justice Young quashed the 28-day sentences that the magistrates gave the couple in September for arrears of £601.48. The couple first appeared in court in August 1992 when they were ordered to pay off their arrears at the rate of £2.00 a week. By the following February, they had paid £256.50 each and were told they had cleared the debt. But in August 1993 they received summonses to reappear in court for £601.48 arrears. They were sentenced in their absence to jail but they won bail pending the judicial review.

Mr Smith's fits have increased to five a day due to the pressure of the court case; his wife, who suffers from rheumatoid arthritis and is asthmatic, has become very withdrawn. A psychiatrist concluded both needed urgent help.

However, the judge refused to award them damages, saying that much of their problem had 'resulted from their uncooperative and aggressive behaviour'. But he took the rare step of ordering the council and the magistrates to share the cost of the couple's legal costs.

The deputy chief executive of the council, said it had followed its statutory duties in attempting to collect the debt. 'Obviously old age and ill-health cannot be reason for not recovering statutory debt,' he said.

(*The Guardian*, 14 December 1993: 3)

It is an interesting exercise to imagine oneself in each of these positions – judge, magistrate, psychiatrist, deputy chief executive and debt collector – and to consider what one would have done in the circumstances.

ourselves. Manufacturers of locks, chains and other security devices have not been slow to trade on such anxieties, but the price we pay is not just financial; we suffer a self-imposed isolation.

Some older people are members of social groups or live in areas that are more vulnerable to crime than others. The headline 'PENSIONER, 82, BURGLED AND BEATEN' is alarmist and irrelevant if the deplorable crime was one in which it was gender, ethnic grouping, locale or household type that had rendered the unfortunate victim vulnerable. There is no link between age and vulnerability to justify this kind of headline. But each time such headlines are published, so the fear of older people grows, so the criminal is tempted to follow the seemingly fruitful and well-trodden path, and so the public tut-tuts apathetically.

If ageing in later life is perceived to be associated with declining value, increasing vulnerability and powerlessness, then the older person may appear a natural victim of modern society. Some commentators, such as the headline writer, may explain seemingly motiveless assault and abuse of older people in this way, and their readers may accept this explanation of how the fate of the unfortunate victims is inevitable given their age. Ageism makes crime tolerable. If older people believe they live in an ageist world in which their well-being is threatened every day, then in an ageist world they live.

Economic dependency

Participation in the labour market still remains a major determinant of status and identity in modern societies. Paid employment grants us activity, mobility, experience and expertise, as well as income. Those who are excluded – children, people over pensionable age, prisoners, the sick – as well as those on the margins – women, the unemployed, older workers, adolescents, the unskilled – live lives in which their freedoms are greatly reduced by their lack of secure and adequate income: most have little to 'bank' on. Most are financially dependent upon members of their families who are not excluded – the economically active – and upon the state. Like the state itself, the economically active are able to exercise power over those who are dependent upon them. This has been the basis of the feminist critique of the organization of the traditional household and the domestic economy: women providing domestic labour are vulnerable to being abused or abandoned.

The moral panic

The balance between the independent economically active and the dependent economically inactive is measured at the national level by the dependency ratio. Defining dependent people as all those under 16 or over 64 years of age, and the independent as all those aged 16 to 64 years, this is the ratio of the numbers of dependent to independent persons in the population. A high value is interpreted as indicating an excessive burden upon the working population, i.e. upon those aged 16 to 64 years. These statistics, however, are defined entirely upon chronological age. The word 'dependency', redolent in ideological significance, represents the assumption that the young and the old are unproductive in an economic sense and therefore dependent upon the productive in-betweenies – the working population.

Sociologists have studied how, in the description of social problems such as immigration and delinquency, media reporting has fostered a moral panic within the public (Hall *et al.* 1978; Cohen 1980). Although it may seem like a new phenomenon, the panic over the burden of an ageing population is in fact an age-old one. Regardless of the actual numbers, there has always been public concern about the 'burden of the aged'. In the seventeenth century, for example, the relief of the elderly poor by the community was a low priority, and in the villages it was often bitterly resented (Thomas 1977: 242). A little more recently, the Royal Commission on Population of 1949 (p. 121) suggested that:

A society in which the proportion of young people is diminishing will become dangerously unprogressive, falling behind other communities not only in technical efficiency and economic welfare, but in intellectual and artistic achievement as well.

(Royal Commission on Population 1949: 121)

This argument is based upon the assumption that the well-being of the nation – whether it be measured by progress, technology, culture or wealth – is directly dependent upon the age distribution of the population, and such arguments are central to institutional and societal ageism. Forty years later, *The Guardian* ran a full page feature on 'The Ageing Population' and its various headlines echoed the fears of the Royal Commission:

A demographic time-bomb to tick away into the next century – This year, Britain will be attempting to grapple with the implications of what has been called the demographic time-bomb – the decline of the British teenager, and the corresponding rise in the proportion of old people in the community.

(*The Guardian*, 2 January 1989: 17)

In many of these reports the primary concern is with the fiscal implications of an increasing population of people dependent upon state funded pensions for their income. Gerontologists have responded to this anxiety with extensive discussions and arguments about the parameters and character of the debate (Johnson *et al.* 1989; Johnson and Falkingham 1992). Jefferys and Thane (1989), for example, focused on service provision and professional groups. They associated the current panic with the publication of government reports concerning service provision, such as *The Rising Tide* (Hospital Advisory Service 1982), and with the professional groups most closely in touch with 'the oldest old' (Jefferys and Thane 1989: 10).

Jefferys is keen to challenge this sense of panic and, in the preface to her book (1989: xiii), suggests that:

the alarm with which the growth in the number of those aged 85 years and over is viewed reflects a deep-seated ambivalence towards older people, which can lead to an exaggeration of the size and nature of the resources required to meet their needs or of the sacrifice required by younger people. It is a matter, we argue, of our sense of values rather than of our capacity to shoulder the burden.

In trying to trace the source of the panic, Walker (1990) identified 'a sense of impending crisis' in a number of international reports issued during the 1980s.

An example came from the Organization for Economic Cooperation and Development:

> The key social policy concern arising out of current demographic trends is whether the ageing of the populations is likely to lead to a major increase in the cost of public social programmes and whether society, and in particular the working population, will be able or willing to bear the additional financing burden.
>
> (OECD 1988: 27)

Walker argues that it is the cost to the government, not the willingness of the working population, that is critical:

> political concern about the cost of ageing has been amplified artificially in order to legitimate policies aimed at diminishing the state's role in financial and social support for older people.
>
> (Walker 1990: 378)

So Walker, unlike Jefferys, sees the panic as having been contrived – if not orchestrated – by the state. He goes on to argue that, in taking action to reduce public expenditure, governments:

> have used the concept of intergenerational equity to legitimate those actions. The result of these will be to widen the division between market-based affluence and publicly administered poverty in old age.
>
> (Walker 1990: 393–4)

A rather different reason to panic? We may do well to panic if we become convinced that intergenerational conflict is being promoted by governments intent upon reductions in public expenditure at all costs. But, if we have confidence that government remains subject to some form of public control, then Jefferys is right in arguing that the basic question rests upon our values and political will. Reviewing the evidence, she concludes:

> It is our values and not our limited means which prevent us from recognizing that our society possesses adequate resources for the task in hand. It is the way in which the public is presented with the facts, rather than the facts themselves, which almost guarantees panic and resistance to the proposal to look for extra resources.
>
> (Jefferys 1989: 12–13)

Adding years to life?

Governmental anxieties about the burden of age have had a powerful effect upon health policies. In the White Paper *The Health of the Nation* (Department of Health 1992), a series of targets has been set. Most of these involve age. The main targets are the following:

Coronary heart disease and stroke

- To reduce death rate for both CHD and stroke in people under 65 by at least 40 per cent by the year 2000.

- To reduce the death rate for CHD in people aged 65–74 by at least 30 per cent by the year 2000.
- To reduce the death rate for stroke in people aged 65–74 by at least 40 per cent by the year 2000.

(Department of Health 1992: 18–19)

People 75 or over are excluded from these three targets even though the White Paper acknowledges that stroke is a major cause of disability 'particularly amongst elderly people' (p. 46). The discussion of charts showing the target in the context of trends in death rates from these causes (p. 48), makes no reference to the fact that they are limited to persons under 65 – a case of older people being invisible and overlooked again.

Cancers

- To reduce the death rate for breast cancer in the population invited for screening by at least 25 per cent by the year 2000.
- To reduce the incidence of invasive cervical cancer by at least 20 per cent by the year 2000.
- To halt the year-on-year increase in the incidence of skin cancer by 2005.
- To reduce the death rate for lung cancer by at least 30 per cent in men under the age of 75 and 15 per cent in women under 75 by 2010.

(Department of Health 1992: 18–19)

Only one of these four targets excludes people aged 75 or over. The first, however, relating to invitations for screening, places a priority on women aged 50 to 64. Likewise, the second draws upon a screening programme with the same priority.

Mental illness

- To improve significantly the health and social functioning of mentally ill people.
- To reduce the overall suicide rate by at least 15 per cent by the year 2000.
- To reduce the suicide rate of severely mentally ill people by at least 33 per cent by the year 2000.

(Department of Health 1992: 18–19)

These targets are not age-specific. In the discussion in the White Paper, however, there is recognition that older people are a vulnerable group with attention in particular being drawn to depression and dementia. Concern is expressed about the prescribing of benzodiazepines to older people. But, again, no targets are set for older people.

HIV/AIDS and sexual health

- To reduce the incidence of gonorrhoea among men and women aged 15–64 by at least 20 per cent by 1995.

- To reduce the rate of conceptions amongst the under 16s by at least 50 per cent by the year 2000.

(Department of Health 1992: 18–19)

There are no targets regarding the sexual health of people over 64. In the White Paper's summary (p. 19), the age band for the first of these targets is omitted, implying an assumption that there is zero risk of gonorrhoea in people under 15 or over 64.

Accidents

- To reduce the death rate for accidents among children aged under 15 by at least 33 per cent by 2005.
- To reduce the death rate for accidents among young people aged 15–24 by at least 25 per cent by 2005.
- To reduce the death rate for accidents among people aged 65 and over by at least 33 per cent by 2005.

(Department of Health 1992: 18–19)

These three targets are all age-specific. Regarding the last of these, the proposed action is as follows:

The Home Office has targeted national television advertising promoting smoke alarm ownership at elderly people and their carers. In 1989 and 1990 a Mobile Unit for the elderly was set up with Age Concern. It toured major urban retail market areas taking the fire safety message to elderly people. It also served to encourage closer co-operation between local fire brigades, Age Concern and other local groups. The Department of Transport has issued a policy document – 'The Older Road User' – which summarises the road safety problems faced by elderly people as drivers, pedestrians and bus passengers and identifies a range of measures for reducing casualties.

As falls are a particularly important cause of accidents amongst older people, the Department of Health will be considering what research might be commissioned into the prevention of falls in elderly people.

(Department of Health 1992: 114)

The Report goes on to consider the relevance of these five key areas for the health of elderly people. It is recognized that preventive measures can be 'just as successful' in older as in younger people (p. 116). Regarding coronary heart disease and stroke in particular, it comments that these are a major cause of ill-health and mortality in older people and that 'effective treatment and rehabilitation services will continue to be vital for the health of elderly people' (p. 118). But such aims are not included in the set targets – people aged 75 or over are excluded.

The overall aim of the strategy outlined in the White Paper is to 'add years to life and life to years' (p. 13). The first of these is linked specifically to a reduction in premature deaths. It is not difficult to see the fifteen main targets listed above as representing the top priority for the health service over the coming ten to twenty years. Eight of these specifically exclude people over 75, and it is likely that older people will have a lower priority than other groups for two others.

Only one target is specific to older people and, in pursuing this objective, the Department of Health is committed to no more than 'considering what research might be commissioned'. It follows that, in seeking to reach these targets, an under-resourced National Health Service will give even less attention to older people than previously. If all the targets are reached, there will have been an increase in life expectation as a result of fewer early deaths. The targets will not be in jeopardy, however, should there be a substantial rise in mortality among older people. Should there be evidence of an improvement in the health levels of older people this will not be as a result of this strategy.

Older car drivers

Preventive measures to reduce accidents often lead to the imposition of prohibitive regulations. The concern to prevent child pedestrian accidents, for example, has led to the installation of security fencing that makes many playgrounds resemble the exercise areas of prisons. It would seem probable that, in order to meet the target of reducing accidents among people aged 65 and over by 33 per cent in the next ten years, the freedom of movement of older people will be restricted. In particular, risks associated with older car drivers will be given detailed attention. Perhaps the target could be achieved at a stroke by insisting that the driving competence of all drivers aged 65 and over is retested.

Imagine an inquiry into the significance of age in the licensing of car drivers. The following is a fictionalized narrative based on an amalgam of a number of published reports.

The inquiry begins with a consultant who has undertaken a review of the literature on traffic accidents and is now reporting to a conference at the Department of Transport. First he has calculated accident rates based on the ages of victims of traffic accidents. This has led to a simple conclusion:

Car drivers aged over 65 have a smaller risk per head of population of being injured than younger drivers.

Perhaps their risk is smaller because they spend less time on the roads? Further analysis of the available statistics has revealed that:

When related to distance driven the risk does increase with age.

The consultant then reports on variations in these statistics between five-year age groups. Injuries and accidents were found to be markedly greater over the age of 70. Armed with these findings he offers a more generalized comment:

The statistics reflect both an increasing vulnerability when elderly people are involved in accidents and a steady decline in their driving skills.

But are these established facts that are being reported or just his own prejudices? His argument proceeds with further statistics:

Their accidents are most likely to occur at junctions when they fail to give way or are making right turns.

Has any research established whether the failure to give way at junctions is age-related? Regarding the question of skill, the consultant now brings into play some scientific knowledge about ability and age:

> *Compared with the capabilities of young drivers, reaction times are longer, information processing is slower, ability to judge the intentions and speed of other drivers may be weaker, and vision may be poorer among elderly drivers.*

The first two of these four assertions are unqualified but the second two include the word 'may'. How certain can we be that older drivers who have accidents have longer reaction times, poorer vision, etc.? Perhaps people who are slower and weaker in these ways – regardless of age – are also more careful? Perhaps the reason why they are more inclined to have accidents is because they are refusing to drive at the speeds of the majority – speeds that are well-known to be dangerous?

However, rather than advocate a general traffic calming strategy such that everyone is safer because everyone has more time to drive carefully – with the outcome that accidents are reduced all round – the consultant proceeds to advocate the provision of advice to elderly people about driving and about when to give up driving. The efforts of the various agencies – the Driver and Vehicle Licensing Authority, general practitioners and motoring organizations – should be coordinated, he argues.

But, someone protests, it is on the basis of this reasoning that special local campaigns have already been mounted to improve road safety, assessing elderly drivers and providing refresher training. These have failed. This only reflects, the consultant argues, the lack of funds for publicity, and the need to work more closely with doctors in providing accurate advice to elderly patients. And so the inquiry goes on.

The consultant's reasoning is a good example of benevolent ageist protectionism. Through an analysis of the incidence of traffic accidents, he seeks to identify methods of control which will reduce accidents. However, the proposed assessment and refresher training, for example, threaten older drivers with humiliation. Moreover, the government will be encouraged to place restrictions upon older drivers. The outcome of this may be that accidents among people aged 65 and over are significantly reduced, and that those among people aged 25 to 64 (interestingly not a target of the Department of Health in regard to the reduction of accidents) increase as average speeds rise with the enforced retirement of older, more cautious, drivers.

Conclusion

In this chapter we have looked at four disparate areas in which power is involved – politics, law, employment and health. I could have picked many more. What is apparent is how closely age is connected to power. It is obvious that power comes to the older individual through the age structuring of institutions and through continuing success in long careers in politics and the professions. Conversely power is exercised upon older people as they increasingly appear to be a drain on limited resources and a burden upon society.

5

The imbecility of old age: The impact of language

The word *imbecility* has great power and, as we will see below, it plays a part in sustaining ageism in the 1990s. There is a tendency, however, to think of ageist language simply in terms of an offensive vocabulary which includes such words. What I hope to do in this chapter is provide some evidence of how it exercises a more subtle power in conversation and public discourse. But first, we begin with words.

Words

It is not difficult to recognize the ageism inherent in terms of abuse such as 'silly old fart'. The word 'old' is widely associated with scorn, fear and vilification. Even when directed at younger people, the repeated use of the word 'old' in such abusive language, often preceded by 'silly' or 'stupid', reinforces the negative associations of age (Nuessel 1984: 274).

The vocabulary of age is particularly rich. There are a number of phonetic roots each of which carry subtly different connotations: age, elder, ger-, old, presby-, senescent, senior. I selected a popular dictionary on sale in the high street, and found that old age itself is given only one definition: 'the later part of life' – simple and inoffensive. In contrast it is itself cited in the definition of eighteen other terms (Bytheway 1993c). Decrepit, for example, is defined as: 'worn out by the infirmities of old age' and senile as: 'showing the decay or imbecility of old age'. Although the aim of a dictionary is to define the meanings of words according to current usage, it also creates meanings through association. The eighteen definitions associate old age with not just imbecility but with a wide range of words that have negative connotations: childishness, decrepit, dotard, dotage, imbecility, infirmities, senility, weakness and worn out.

In recent times, the word 'elderly' has acquired a certain predominance in gerontology, and in social policy and care literature. What characteristic is it that elderly people share? Often a working definition is offered: 'In this report we will define elderly people as those over 75 years of age.' This kind of statement certainly clears the air but why use the word 'elderly'? Why not 'the over-75s'? Just as 'Brown, 45' represents reference to age in mass journalism, so elderly has become institutionalized in these more specialized literatures. It has certain appealing ideological connotations: a certain deference that one associates with elders, for example. The word 'elder' carries with it a sense of respect, dignity and – perhaps most important – power and authority: 'our elders and betters', 'elder statesmen'. Terms such as 'village elders' and 'the elders of the tribe' often allude to distant places where older people are thought to be properly respected. Irrespective of the truth about these claims, such observations may be all part and parcel of our sense of guilt regarding the way 'our society treats its elders'.

Whatever the origin, it is certainly the case that the word 'elderly' is now used less discerningly. It is almost invariably a blanket reference to all those over a certain age, typically 65 or 75. Through its loose association with respect, and in its flexibility regarding the specification of the category, it is both positive and euphemistic.

As was shown in Chapter 4, emotive words are frequently used to promote the moral panic over age: the demographic time-bomb; the silent epidemic of dementia; a plague of wrinklies; the rising tide; the grey hordes – such phrases directly imply that an ageing population threatens family, community and nation alike. I ended Chapter 4 with a critical word in the vocabulary of ageism: 'burden'. Warnes, in an exhaustive study of the origins and associations of this word reports that it is now 'rampant in the social science and humanities literature' (1993: 318). He goes on to say:

> Few gerontologists would dispute that the legitimate efforts of fiscal analysts and policy makers to draw attention to the monetary burdens of old age income support have enormously influenced for ill the public perception of the well-being and deservedness of elderly people. Comparable and unpredictable damage may occur with the dissemination of simplified understandings of care through the terminology and points of view of care-giver burden research. The history of burden shows that coarsened and simplified social constructions can become rampant and do great damage.
>
> (Warnes 1993: 328)

What is happening is that language is being used in policy literature to place the blame for social problems upon those who suffer the consequences. It is as though 'the elderly' are a group of people who have conspired to place this burden upon 'us'.

Coupland *et al.* (1991: 16) have called for further, more sophisticated research into the connotations of age terms:

> Our interpretation of the significance of these usages, and the extent to which we do in fact need to view them as ageist, depends on this more sophisticated approach.

While there is no doubting the need for continued research into the power of language, the idea that a sophisticated assessment is needed of 'the extent to which we do in fact need to view' expressions of scorn and ridicule as ageist, seems excessively cautious. It is not the role of researchers to be prescriptive: placing the seal of approval upon those terms shown to be non-ageist. The priority of linguistic research *should* be on the relationship between terminology, the categorization of people and the production of negative stereotypes. It is interesting to note, for example, how in the quotes included on pages 47 and 50, both Chen Yun and British judges are described as 'old and out of touch'.

Abusive and emotive words are an important component of ageist language. However, to appreciate just how age-sensitive modern society has become, one must listen to ordinary everyday conversation.

Conversation

RA's interview with the two receptionists (page 7), is a good example of how self-conscious people can be over revealing their age. Coupland *et al.* (1991) have studied conversations between younger and older people. They analysed a number of typical extracts that had been transcribed precisely as spoken. They refer to two as illustrating ageism. In one, the older woman says:

> And I'm, I'm not very well these days too. I'm seventy last October. So I, I find I can't do it so good.
>
> (Coupland *et al.* 1991: 137–8)

And in the other, the younger woman says to the older woman who has just revealed she is 77:

> I thought you were sort of 60 I just assumed . . . it's funny, most people I know who are 77 aren't [gasps] dashing in and out of day centres.
>
> (ibid. 143–4)

What both examples illustrate is how people in ordinary conversation regularly associate actual chronological ages with precisely drawn expectations. The 77-year-old clearly indicates that her age limits her capabilities. If challenged she might accept that it is her state of health and fitness that is the immediate constraint, but this would not negate the fact that, through the ageist beliefs she has acquired over a long life, she ascribes her incapacities to age. Likewise, if the younger woman were to be challenged as to who precisely these 77-year-olds are who are mostly not dashing in and out of day centres, she may be a little embarrassed to admit that she doesn't know. Nevertheless, what she does – and presumably will continue to do – is evoke her experience of age-specific behaviours in these terms, when patronizingly admiring the achievements of the exceptions to the rule.

A doctor's receptionist in a recorded conversation described the problems she faces in giving access to the doctor to those patients most in need. The following is a transcription of her account. Alongside a sensitive and admirable

---

The 'Richards' dress

The following is part of a conversation between two lecturers that was overheard in a university common room in 1988:

A: That's a nice dress.

B: Oh, I've rather gone off it. It's the sort of dress that's suitable for visiting your mother in . . .

A: Oh, I think it looks nice.

B: Well, it's a Richards dress you see, and I keep seeing people in it all over the place – all these 60-year-olds. It's really put me off!

No offensive words are used, but ageism is clearly apparent. You might consider what would have happened if the person overhearing the conversation had interjected: 'Don't be so ageist!' What might A have said? What might B have felt? What if the interjector was someone who looked about 60 years of age?

---

concern for the patient, there is the benevolent 'new ageism' described by Kalish (1979):

You find more of the elderly, they're afraid to come because they think they are bothering the doctor. A lot of people, they phone in and their cards are very thin, and perhaps they're about 80. They've only seen the doctor once or twice, and they've got to ring in for an appointment for a doctor to call, and you can tell they are really ill, they are desperate or they wouldn't do it, you know. I think a lot of people are afraid to come, you know, so I think perhaps sort of a letter to . . . Well I suppose they cover the old ones now don't they? But then again a lot of over-75s they don't want the nurses to call . . . You know, they sort of think it's tempting fate. I think a lot of them do, don't they? They won't come to the doctors, just in case. If they feel OK they won't bother. So I think a lot of oldies don't want to know . . . A lot of them, the old ones that haven't come before, they say, 'Oh, you know, I hope I'm not going to have a run now', because they haven't been for years, and then they've got to come because there's something wrong. And then they worry. It's like if they think they come to the doctors and then they're going to find something then. So they, I think a lot of them tend to think, they won't bother, you know. They feel OK so they're not going to tempt fate [laugh] . . . I think that the elderly ones always sort of think, am I, am I desperate then, whereas a younger one will just come.

There is one particularly significant way in which grammar can amplify ageism within conversation. When being introduced to a stranger and being asked who you are and what you do, with age you tend to answer with accounts of what you were and what you used to do. What you are is a 'former' this, a 'retired' that or an 'ex-' the other. Even when you answer positively with a statement of what you are currently spending your time doing, the question remains hanging in the air. The sensitive stranger is perhaps reluctant to ask what you used to do and so the significant past remains unrevealed. On occasions however, work identities survive long after the work itself is left behind. When I met John Evans of Llewitha, Swansea, aged 111 years, he still called himself a miner, proud of the sixty years he had spent working underground.

Humour

I have two collections of cartoons, each a series of indications of when you become old. The first is a collection called *Over The Hill* (Ivory Tower 1988). Of 46 cartoons, 34 are directed at men, nine at women and three at couples. The second is called *Old is . . . Great!* (Markham 1978). It includes 56 cartoons, all featuring the same heroine. There are certain common themes in these jokes:

1 Failing eyesight:
   Old is . . . when candlelit tables are no longer romantic because you can't read the menu.
   You're over the hill when . . . you find yourself squinting during candlelit dinners.

2 Reduced frequency of sexual activity:
   Old is . . . when you can't remember the last time you had sex with your husband and your husband can't remember either.
   You're over the hill when . . . you still feel your youthful ardour but only once in a while.

3 Failing memory:
   Old is . . . when you can't remember the original colour of your own hair.
   You're over the hill when . . . sometimes you stop to think and forget to start again.

Both collections, however, include a number of obliquely positive messages:

Old is . . . when you look in the mirror and think to yourself 'Aren't I wise?'

You're over the hill when . . . you have a very special comfortable chair from which it is very difficult to remove you.

These contrast with a more overtly ageist collection, *Geriatrics: A Selection of Bad Taste Cartoons* (Silvey-Jex 1980). Most of these revolve around incapacity: the hospital patient who has forgotten to take his pyjama trousers down before sitting on the toilet; inappropriate walking sticks – too short, too flexible, too collapsible; continence bottles; walking frame relays; dust and cobwebs; and so on.

Age, like gender and race, has always been the base of much derogatory humour. It is sometimes justified as laughing at ourselves but the reality is often humiliating for older people. Weber and Cameron (1978) reviewed three American studies that had found that between 56 per cent and 66 per cent of jokes published in anthologies about age were adjudged to be negative. They argued, however, that the methodologies that the three researchers had used were weak and that it is difficult to judge what is negative and what is positive. All three researchers responded to these criticisms, all agreeing that their methodologies could be improved and that judgement was problematic, but asserting nevertheless that the ageism in jokes should be challenged:

> Just as we have become more aware of and sensitive to racism and sexism wearing the mask of 'humour' about blacks and women, I think a greater awareness of ageism in humour would be a healthy thing for us as individuals and as a society.
>
> (Palmore 1978: 76)

> When comedians and joke tellers are not from the group who is the brunt of the joke, an in-group versus out-group effect is established. For example, male comedians who define an Old Maid as 'a woman who's been good for nothing' convey an 'in-group' attitude (male) about an out-group (never-married females).
>
> (Davies 1978: 76–7)

In general what all age-based humour does is establish and reinforce the stereotypes of old age – even the more positive – and, like birthday cards, threaten the reader with the possibility of recognizing their own characteristics and circumstances. The question of whether they are negative or positive is important but not critical.

Betty Spital, like the more famous Dame Edna Everage, is a comic creation that challenges our expectations of older women. The teasing question her humour poses is: is she ageist or anti-ageist? She is introduced as 'Pensioner Activist and Radical Granny' and General Secretary of the Sheffield Pensioners' Liberation Army Faction (SPLAF):

> Pankhurst dubbed her 'an inspiration', Marx called her '*mein schpitalischgefreund*', while to Pablo Picasso she was known simply as 'Hots'.
>   Her contribution to the political life of Steel City is legendary. Few will forget the SPLAF sponsored streak against hypothermia, nor the one-woman crusade to legalise Youthenasia – a pensioner's right to choose which of her or his offspring to have put down.
>
> (Meade 1987)

This introduction presents Betty Spital as a historical figure with contacts and experiences that her younger radical colleagues can only wonder at, as someone who can mobilize massive political power and through this threaten the lives of the younger generation. This is what she has to say about ageism:

> Ageism. It's a terrible thing. Not nice at all. And my comrades and I of SPLAF will not cease in our struggle to have this scourge obliterated from the face of the earth. Intolerance against others purely on the grounds of age is disgraceful, and I'll not tolerate it!
>   You may think me outspoken on this one, but it's a matter on which I feel strongly; just because some people are unfortunate enough to be under 60 is no reason to despise them.
>
> (Meade 1987: 14)

Setting to one side the satire, this commentary conveys both a political correctness in being against all oppressive 'isms' and, again, Spital's confidence in her ability to wield power and patronage.

One would like to think that Betty Spital was indeed a grandmother and pensioner, a member of the 'in-group' (Davies 1978), but in the credits at the end of the book we are introduced to Jane Baker: 'In a kind light she bears a marked resemblance to Betty Spital . . . Jane is due to retire in 1997.' Is it acceptable then for a person of presumably 52 years of age to adopt the persona of Betty Spital and to launch this attack upon ageism? By claiming to be Betty who is 'in', is Jane (who arguably is 'out') being offensive to grandmothers and pensioners? And if so, is it then necessarily ageist, or might it be an incisive challenge to the absurdity of these social categorizations?

Advertisements

It is often said that modern advertising is ageist in that it rarely features older people, even when they constitute a large segment of a product's market: bath soaps, for example. It is perhaps more blatantly ageist, however, when it exploits age stereotypes.

A particularly choice example of this was a full-page advertisement that appeared in the national newspapers in December 1993. A woman dressed as a caricature of older women – an old-fashioned dress, gloves, handbag, wrinkled stockings – is sitting with her back to a blank wall. Next to her is a side table on which there is a small decorated box. Below this image there is the slogan: 'This Christmas, shoot Granny and put her in a box.' There is a look of alarm on her face.

The text that follows promotes the product – a range of cameras packaged in gift sets. It adopts the aggressive and sarcastic style of humour that is associated with the stereotyped yuppie. For example: 'You can capture Christmas Day as it actually deteriorates. You can snap the toys before the little angels do.' This attempt at humour would, one presumes, be used to defend the slogan and the opening sentence, the only further reference to 'Granny': 'She won't even have time to put her teeth in.'

The Guardian subsequently published two complaints about this advertisement – under the less than serious cover title 'Boxing clever' (*The Guardian*, 30 December 1993). One correspondent commented upon the 'implied violence', the other on the 'ridiculing of elderly women'.

The camera gift set was being targeted upon a younger market through the use of ageist humour. Ageism is also clearly apparent in advertisements that heighten anxieties about ageing. Over the years, the cosmetics industry has consistently capitalized upon this and there is a wide range of products, mostly targeted at women, which claim success in defying age:

Medical science discovers brilliant new anti-ageing cream . . . Will renew ageing skin, reduce wrinkles and revitalize your appearance to look years younger . . . Without this vital process your skin will become aged, dry and wrinkled . . . So now you can face every day of the rest of your life looking years younger!

The sensitive skin around your eyes is often among the first areas of your face to show signs of early ageing. The skin in this area is very thin and is more vulnerable to the ravages of ageing . . . X finally brings to a halt the ageing process around your eyes . . . Within days you will look years younger.

Banish ugly ageing skin blemishes . . .

Cosmetic chemists develop instant way to look years younger . . . Takes years off your face in minutes. Just wipe on – peel off – you'll be amazed . . . Sagging jowls will be firmed up . . . Now you don't have to look your age any longer . . . You will again have the confidence to look in the mirror – and your friends will notice how much younger you look and will wonder how you do it!

These messages make direct links between the ageing process and appearance: the 'ravages' of the former lead to dry, wrinkled, sagging, ugly, blemished skin. The various 'anti-ageing' products reverse the process: skin is renewed, wrinkles reduced, appearance revitalized, jowls firmed up, and all these products guarantee that 'you will look years younger'.

Positive images?

Despite older people constituting a large section of the consumer market, very few products are advertised directly through a positive image of later life. An exception is Jack Daniel's Tennessee Whiskey. One advertisement in a series that focuses upon its long history and traditional methods, portrays Herb Fanning at his local bar. It reads:

Tough old birds like Herb Fanning here are why you'll continue to find Jack Daniel's so smooth. Mr Fanning has held every job in our Hollow. So he knows his whiskey inside out. And though he's long retired these days, we occasionally bring him back to check on things. You see, we know there's a certain rareness you've come to expect in Jack Daniel's. We can't risk changing that. And with prideful watchdogs like Herb on the scene, we don't think we ever will.

Definitely patronizing, this nevertheless acknowledges the power of experience and, more particularly, the value that is placed upon such experience in the spirits market.

In 1991, Fuji, the photographic film manufacturers, ran an advertising campaign that dealt not just with ageism but also with disablism and racism. It included a positive image of an older couple. Unlike the example of Tennessee whiskey, there was no connection between the respective qualities of the couple and Fuji's product. The campaign created a huge response and much debate. Despite the positive and challenging messages being conveyed, there was a feeling that vulnerable groups were being exploited in the promotion of a commercial product. As with the more infamous Benetton campaigns, it was suspected by some that Fuji was only interested in achieving favourable publicity for itself. Despite this, Fuji and their advertising agents, contrasting their advertisements with those that exploit women in familiar and discredited ways, insisted that their campaign promoted human dignity:

> Socially aware advertising can make a real contribution to an improved society, a true reflection on the way that people are able to live their lives, not a synthetic picture constructed by the media for popular consumption.
> (Goldsmith 1991: 16)

There are important issues raised by Fuji's initiative. If their only objective is profit, then all their philanthropic efforts should be discredited. If, however, we remember that the individual executive is a person with ordinary human concerns, we might suppose these will occasionally override the narrow pursuit of profit. It could still be argued that a campaign which helps to sustain a good public image for Fuji is working to this end – just as much as the advertisement which claims that Fuji makes high quality film. But we should not underestimate the extent to which individual executives within such a firm do battle over issues such as advertising strategies. Arguably the Fuji initiative was a triumph for one honourable individual who believed that she/he was in a situation in which critical social issues concerning age could and should be given a high-profile public airing. Even if the dominant message of a particular moral image is not 100 per cent satisfactory, better that than the alternative of an image which is not quite 100 per cent immoral. Perhaps if more people individually took advantage of their particular situations and exercised their limited power to raise such issues and to challenge oppressive aspects of the prevailing ethos, and in particular to confront ageism, perhaps then the quality of all our lives might be raised a little.

Journalism

Advertisements are a well-known channel of ageism in the media. Less familiar is the case of journalism. The phrase 'dozens of octogenarians and septuagenarians lurking in the half-light behind the official power structure' that appeared in the 17 October 1992 story on the resignation of the Chinese 'old guard' (page 47) seems distinctly offensive. There is, of course, something xenophobic about the report, but we might also ask whether there are also dozens of sexagenarians and quinquagenarians who similarly lurk.

Defying age is one example of the heroics that sports journalists regularly feature. Their praise represents a certain kind of benevolent ageism that celebrates the achievements of those of great age. The following is an example of the patronage of older professional footballers:

> There are times when watching Leeds that you half expect a strident voice to rise above the crowd like a guide leading tourists around an ancient building. 'And this is McClelland, a remarkable example of preservation. And to your right Strachan, a restoration jewel. And above, Chapman, an extraordinary architectural oddity . . .' One startling moment on Saturday saw McClelland, 35, give the terrier-sharp Saunders, 27, a yard start and beat the Welshman for pace. Faced with such improbable happenings, it is impossible not to marvel at the fabric of Howard Wilkinson's team. Yet the

nagging question remains: very nice now, but will it eventually collapse? Five of the team are thirty-something, to be joined by Sterland next week. Towards the end of last season, as the fixtures clustered ever closer, venerable and vulnerable legs began to creak and shriek. The pattern is in danger of being repeated.

(*The Guardian*, 23 September 1991)

Much wittier than the camera advertisement, this is not untypical of the approach of sports journalists to age. In my view it articulates the following ageist expectations:

- McClelland, Strachan and Chapman had no reasonable right to expect to be on the field;
- it is not because of skill but preservation, restoration and eccentricity that they are;
- age is expected to determine speed and we cannot expect September successes in challenging this expectation to continue to the end of the season – there is evidence from last season that older legs do not last;
- half the team is over 30 years of age – Wilkinson would be well advised to promote some younger players.

Images

Although we tend to think of images as visual phenomena, they are often transmitted through the written word. The words of Godlove *et al.* (page 4), for example, evoke unambiguously a particularly appalling image. As in this book, words are often accompanied by visual images.

Over the last ten years or so, much has been written about the image of age. The idea that it masks an ageless person is now well known (Featherstone and Hepworth 1993). Ageism provides a basis for reacting negatively to the mask, interpreting it in terms of stereotyped images. These stereotyped images are often used in advertisements (as described above) and in this way they reinforce and disseminate cultural aspects of ageism. In this section, I want to consider the image we present in public places and how sometimes we might attempt to organize this in ways related to age.

One of the critical challenges most of us face in managing our ageing is that of sustaining a sense of continuity. We all acquire an acute sense of our public image and, in particular, of the ways in which this might align us with a particular generation or age group (see page 5). Most of us want to be either in fashion or dressing appropriately for our age; either way this means being sensitive to trends in dress and appearance. But most of the time we also want to remain recognizably the same person we have always been.

The mirror

As the cosmetics manufacturers are well aware, we examine the image in the mirror whenever we dress and prepare to face the world. We return our gaze and every so often the question of age is addressed (Woodward 1991). Etta Clark for example, wrote: 'The biggest surprise of my life was on my fortieth birthday when I glanced into a mirror and saw an older woman squinting back' (1986: vii).

Consider also what Barbara Macdonald says about her face:

My hair is grey, white at the temples, with only a little of the red cast of earlier years showing through. My face is wrinkled and deeply lined. Straight lines have formed on the upper lip as though I had spent many years with my mouth pursed. This has always puzzled me and I wonder what years those were and why I can't remember them. My face has deep lines that extend from each side of the nose down the face past the corners of my mouth. My forehead is wide, and the lines across my forehead and between my eyes are there to testify that I was often puzzled and bewildered for long periods of time about what was taking place in my life. My cheekbones are high and become more noticeably so as my face is drawn further and further down. My chin is small for such a large head and below the chin the skin hangs in a loose vertical fold from my chin all the way down my neck, where it meets a horizontal scar.

(Macdonald and Rich 1983: 13–14)

Both Clark and Macdonald are facing the reality of the age and the image of the person in the mirror. From time to time many of us thinking, like Clark, of this as another person, express surprise at an apparent change, 'How come all of a sudden I'm that older person?' At other times, like Macdonald, we inspect the face and wonder how it came to be as it is. At the beginning of most days we prepare the image in the mirror for an appearance in public and this can entail extensive manipulations, many of which are designed to sustain the image of a younger self. In a markedly patriarchal world, this is particularly true for women. As Arber and Ginn have argued, power over women is exercised through the promotion of a youthful sexualized image (1991: 42). The following is an extract from Sontag's famous 1972 *Saturday Review* article:

A woman's face is potentially separate from her body. She does not treat it naturalistically. A woman's face is the canvas upon which she paints a revised, corrected portrait of herself. One of the rules of this creation is that the face does not show what she doesn't want it to show. Her face is an emblem, an icon, a flag.

(Sontag 1978: 78)

How does this cosmetic image relate to age? Does it simply present a sexualized youth or is it more subtle than that? Women working in gerontology are in a good position to express a view. One commented:

My views about dyeing my hair are interesting in the sense that they reveal my attempts to deny my ageing. As a woman I still feel a strong sense to conform to a view of myself as 'young and attractive' that was formed many years ago. I admit that I have internalized my image so now I don't feel like myself without my eye make-up on . . . I know for a fact that it adds to my self-confidence in certain situations.

So is Sontag right that the face in the mirror is waiting to be recreated, or is the gerontologist simply trying to maintain a continuity in her image in

Properly constituted social beings
Hirwaun Primary School; Gregory James

defiance of physical ageing? Is it not the case that once we start using cosmetic means to disguise the visible effects of ageing, we are immediately threatened by the increasing divergence between appearance and reality: the longer we continue to sustain a particular 'false' image, the greater the change in appearance that will follow a decision to revert to reality?

What we confront in the mirror is largely the face and, as Macdonald and Sontag demonstrate, it is the naked face that commands attention. Nevertheless, in the production of public images, we have to attend to other parts of the body and also to dress and equip ourselves to function as properly constituted social beings. In anticipation of the public gaze, we consciously prepare our bodies: hair, make-up, spectacles, clothes, shoes; and we do this through: washing, shaving, perfuming, painting, clipping, brushing, polishing, dressing, checking and straightening. And, before launching ourselves into the public arena, we check our image in the mirror once again before composing ourselves and stepping forth.

It is often when this public image contrasts conspicuously with the more private image of the unprepared body that age is most apparent. An Aberdeen woman gave Rory Williams the following powerful description of the contrasting images that her husband presents:

> I sometimes – I look at him when he's sleeping, and I think, 'Gosh, you're getting old.' Especially with this chest, because his mouth's not closed during the night, you see. I sometimes stand over him and just look, you know; and his mouth's open and he's maybe lying on his back if he's snoring, and his hair's grey . . . I just hope he doesn't do the same with me . . . (laughing) . . . Because I don't tell him. And I just think, 'Oh, Edward,' you know, 'What a shame, poor Edward' with this breathing. And he's so nice and so gay and so good, you know, a lovely kind person. It makes me sad. Then in the morning he comes down all dressed up with his fancy tie and his nice suit on . . .
>
> (Williams 1990: 71)

Books

Books are an important channel of communication and, although their dominant medium is the written word, pictures and other visual images are particularly important in conveying messages and constructing or challenging stereotyped images of later life. In this book, I have included a number of illustrations. A photograph presents an image. At one level it is of a particular person, born on a certain date in a particular place and photographed at a particular time in a particular place. At another level, it is an image that is selected for inclusion. It is always difficult to establish what a chosen image actually conveys. As you look at each and examine the image in detail, you begin to wonder whether the image is promoting a stereotyped or an idiosyncratic image of later life.

A quite extraordinary demonstration of the power of ageist imagery is to be found in a textbook for nurses on the care of older people (Redfern 1986). An illustrative figure is composed of three photographs and captioned 'Young and old skin'. The text which immediately precedes reference to this figure reads:

> The ability for light to pass through skin (transparency) increases with age in both sexes. Wrinkles are closely associated with age changes in the dermis and both aged skin and sun-damaged skin lose tone and elasticity giving rise to sagging and wrinkling.
>
> (Redfern 1986: 41)

Given this, you might expect to be offered three comparable illustrations of young, old and sun-damaged skin. What is published, however, is the head and shoulders of a woman facing the camera, probably in her twenties, with a good complexion and wearing a necklace and dress; the head and shoulders of an older man, perhaps 70, seemingly undressed and looking to his left; and a rear view of the naked buttocks and testicles of an older man – perhaps the same man.

If the intention is to illustrate the contrast between young and old skin, it seems astonishing that the author should choose these three images. The first two would have sufficed, although even then the age comparison would have been confounded with gender and posture. Moreover, two closer photographs of the skin of forearms, say, may have better illustrated the caption. If the image of bare buttocks is relevant, then surely two contrasting images of young and old buttocks would have been necessary?

There must have been a reason for these three photographs to be included. Even allowing for the possibility of last minute problems in the availability of preferred alternatives, it seems probable that the selection will have been justified in the following way:

> The typical reader is a young trainee nurse. She needs to be shocked with the sight of the elderly body. She should be made to realize, early on in this textbook, that nursing elderly people is not all sweetness and light, that it involves much unseemly body work. For this reason we'll include this photograph of naked buttocks and testicles. This is a good place since we are discussing sagging and wrinkled skin.

If this is the case, then the decision is ageist in the way in which it is intended to associate unattractive work with nursing older people. One also wonders if the patient's permission was obtained for his bare buttocks and testicles to be published in a textbook.

Conclusion

This chapter has included many examples of how language and image relate to ageism. Overall there are two complementary threads. One is the distancing of older people: those people perceived to be elderly, to suffer innumerable problems and to have wrinkled, sagging bodies. Through the grammar of language it is so easy to set them apart and to feel divorced from their miserable lives. The second thread, reflecting upon the undeniable truths that once they were younger and that we too will be older, is for language to articulate a sense of anxiety, fear and panic. It is the potential for words to become emotive that represents the power of language.

6

Get your knickers off, granny: Interpersonal relations

Age is an individual characteristic and when strangers meet there is often a certain sensitivity, if not curiosity, about each other's age. But age is also the basis for characterizing the relationship between two people. This may be articulated in terms of generational membership: 'I'm talking about my generation not yours . . .', but this is often referred to as an age difference. The ways in which people interrelate to this difference is a critical element of ageism: 'When you are my age, you'll understand!'

In this chapter, I raise a number of issues regarding the different contexts in which two people might relate to each other. Although other people might also be involved – for example, filial relations normally involve two parents and a number of children – I want to concentrate on how just two people might interrelate and, in particular, how their relationship might be affected by ageism.

Birthdays

We experience age most directly and unambiguously on our birthdays. Birthdays are celebrated every twelve months throughout our lives – and beyond. They are not just a registering of our increasing age but also a reason, an excuse, for a party – whether through a feast of ox and camel (as in the case of the ancient Persians), a visit to the local pizzeria, or a special meal at home with family and friends. For many of us the party is planned and arranged by others. On the eve of her 79th birthday, for example, May Sarton wrote in her diary: 'I've been opening about thirty cards and letters. Wonderful to hear from friends old and new' (Sarton 1993: 341).

Birthdays can also, of course, be distressingly negative experiences. We are all threatened by the possibility of a birthday that no one remembers, the humiliation of the one birthday card that in truth you bought for yourself.

Today is my birthday

The following extracts are taken from Brett (1987). They variously reflect how physical changes in the body and social relations determine the individual's response to a birthday.

- John Evelyn, a wealthy royalist, in 1702, four years before his death, acknowledging God's mercy:

  Arriv'd now to the 82nd year of my age, having read over all that pass'd since this day twelvemonth in these notes, I render solemn thanks to the Lord, imploring the pardon of my past sins, and the assistance of His grace; making new resolutions, and imploring that He will continue His assistance, and prepare me for my blessed Saviour's coming, that I may obtain a comfortable departure, after so long a term as has ben hitherto indulg'd me. I find by many infirmities this yeare (especially nephritic pains) that I much decline; and yet of His infinite mercy retain my intellects and senses in greate measure above most of my age.

- Byron, writing with a 'heaviness of heart' on the eve of his birthday in 1821:

  Through life's road, so dim and dirty,
  I have dragged to three-and-thirty,
  What have these years left to me?
  Nothing – except thirty-three.

- Elizabeth Barrett reflecting on the death of her mother in 1832 on her 26th birthday:

  My birthday! – My thoughts will go to the past – the past – to the ever ever beloved! My happy days went away with her!

- Two entries that Queen Victoria made in her diary, first in 1833:

  Today it is my 18th birthday! How old! and yet how far am I from being what I should be. I shall from this day take the *firm* resolution to study with renewed assiduity, to keep my attention always well fixed on whatever I am about, and to strive to become every day less trifling and more fit for what, if Heaven wills it, I'm some day to be!

and then in 1900:

  Again my old birthday returns, my eighty-first! . . . The number of telegrams to be opened and read was quite enormous, and obliged six men to be sent for to help the two telegraphists in the house. The answering of them was an interminable task, but it was most gratifying to receive so many marks of loyalty and affection.

- Chips Channon, writing in 1934, the year before he became Conservative MP for Southend:

> My 35th birthday. Actually I have lied so much about my age that I forget how old I really am. I think I look 28, and know I feel 19.
>
> ● Harold Nicolson, diplomat and journalist, writing in 1946, offering a particularly pessimistic view of his physical state:
>
> I reach the age of sixty. Until about five years ago I detected no decline at all in physical vigour and felt as young as I did at thirty. In the last five years, however, I am conscious that my physical powers are on the decline.
>
> ● Peter Hall, theatre director, in 1976:
>
> Forty-six today; fifty in sight. The good thing I suppose is that I have reached a point most people reach in their fifties rather than their forties so I reckon I can sit out the swing of fashion against me. But I am doing too much.

A magazine article on 'The Great British Tantrum' begins with an account of how Keith Floyd, the television gourmet, threw one on 28 December 1992:

> He was having an awful birthday. For one thing it was his 49th, which in anybody's language means 50 and the last stages of decrepitude staring you in the face. For another, it fell only three days after the rest of the world . . . had given up on the idea of celebrating anything . . . 'I know it sounds childish and ridiculous, but when your birthday is a few days after Christmas, nobody ever bothers to buy you a birthday present. It is something that has got to me ever since I was a little boy.'
>
> (*The Independent Magazine*, 9 January 1993: 14)

Conversely we are also threatened by the more humiliating or unwelcome aspects of a positive response: the unwanted gifts, the fuss, the mess, the unconvincing expressions of affection, and so on. Betty Friedan provides an account of how ageism spoilt the celebration of her sixtieth birthday:

> When my friends threw a surprise party on my sixtieth birthday, I could have killed them all. Their toasts seemed hostile, insisting as they did that I publicly acknowledge reaching sixty, pushing me out of life, as it seemed, out of the race. Professionally, politically, personally, sexually. Distancing me from their fifty, forty, thirty-year-old selves.
>
> (Friedan 1993: xiii)

Birthday cards

The most public manifestation of the culture surrounding birthdays is the card and, increasingly during the 1980s and 1990s, the cards available for purchase in the high street are openly ageist.

During the 1970s, following Butler's work on ageism, some systematic attention was paid by American gerontologists to ageism and humour, and one

Birthday cards
Photograph: Roger Davies

of these studies looked at birthday cards (Demos and Jache 1981). In an analysis of 496 humorous birthday cards, 195 (39 per cent) were found to have an ageing theme. These were then judged by three independent judges and, where there was consensus, 80 per cent were considered negative. Of the 195 cards, 55 per cent dealt with physical or mental characteristics – rather more negatively than positively, particularly in regard to appearance and sexuality. The authors concluded that these cards reinforced ageist ideas.

Less ambitiously, on the day before the 1989 British Society of Gerontology conference, I visited a large stationery shop in Swansea and examined the 'humorous' birthday cards that were on display. In a period of fifteen minutes, I selected and purchased 16 cards which I considered to be clear examples of ageism. These I displayed at the conference under four headings, and the following are examples which reflect upon the relationship between the giver and the receiver of the card:

1 Messages about changes in physical appearance (six cards)

I think birthday cards that take the
mickey out of getting old are just
cruel, and *insensitive* . . .   . . . what do you think *crinkle-
                                                        chops?!!!*

When I told someone it was your
birthday they said you were *old and
wrinkly* but I defended you . . .   . . . I said you weren't that wrinkly!

2 Messages about physical weakness and failures in sexual performance (four
cards)

Now you're getting older, *sex* is like a
veteran car . . .   . . . it only comes out once a year . . .
                                                 and even then it has to be hand
                                                 started!

3 Humiliating messages about the undesirability of old age (four cards)

If you think I sent you this *card* just
because its your birthday, you're
wrong . . .   . . . it's also out of respect for the
                                                 elderly!

4 Messages about incapacity (two cards)

Cards which make fun about
people's age are in bad taste . . .   . . . anyway while you can read this
                                                 tiny print you're still young! [printed
                                                 in large letters]

Gibson (1993) also studied British birthday cards and concluded that they
are 'examples of aggressive ageism, often combined with sexism' containing
'crude jokes about the coming of old age with all its supposed horrors'. These
kinds of cards are part of an increasing tendency to turn birthdays into an
occasion for public humiliation. Apart from the sending of cards, the victims
also encounter messages on their way to work daubed on sheets hanging over
pedestrian bridges and then, on their return, the outside of their homes
festooned, not just with balloons and flags, but with public declarations of
name and age. There follow alcoholic parties featuring offensive jokes,
kissograms and other kinds of sexual humiliation. While this kind of
experience is not universal, it provides a clear indication of how age is
important in interpersonal relations, and how birthdays can be used as a means
of reinforcing this significance.

Filial relations

Much ageism is bound up in the relationship between children and parents.
The generation gap has been a favourite media topic for many years. Typically
this centres upon the crises associated with the end of childhood. Children are
expected to assume adult responsibilities and to adopt aspirations set by their
parents, and the parents feel threatened with rolelessness after many years of
full-time parenthood. In this situation, the conflicts are often articulated in
terms of each other's age:

*Don't you talk to me like that! When I was your age, I knew how to respect my
parents!*

countered by:

> *You're so boring! Things have moved on since your day! You won't find me being so old-fashioned when I'm your age!*

And so it goes on, moving rapidly into wilder assertions about each other's generation. In this way a powerful generation-specific and mutually reinforcing form of ageism develops.

Migration

Gruman (1978) has provided a vivid description of the tensions that develop between generations in the context of immigration. He describes how the USA at the time of Theodore Roosevelt was dominated by a reverence of youth. This affected, in particular, the families of those people who arrived in America between 1880 and 1924:

> Mostly young, they nevertheless rapidly became the lost generation viewed, with remarkable unanimity, as expendable in the securing of a beach-head for the next, Americanized generation. With the arrival of the first child in school, the family order was dramatically reversed as the young took the key role of mediator between home and society.
>
> (Gruman 1978: 366)

One can recognize similarities between this and the experience of immigrants to Britain in the immediate post-war period. Blakemore and Boneham (1993: 36–7), for example, suggest that intergenerational conflict is increased when younger generations feel themselves being pushed into a caste-like status, while the older generation remains set in an immigrant identity dreaming of a home they never return to.

The child–parent relationship changes as both age, and as they each interpret their respective passages through life. If I were to attempt an archetypal account of this experience I might suggest that the parent initially seems relatively un-ageing as the small child grows rapidly taller and taller, changing from an infant of a few inches to an adult, often taller than the parents themselves. But, as the child settles into a static sense of adulthood, both begin to recognize that the parent has been ageing as well and that the parent is now becoming vulnerable to the vicissitudes of time.

This normative biography suits the ideological view that parents should have prime (if not sole) responsibility for the dependent child, and therefore that we should enter into parenthood at an age when we are best able to meet the commitments perceived as extending over twenty or more years of life. In time the independent adult-child takes on prime (if not sole) responsibility for the dependent 'aged' parent.

Post-menopausal pregnancy

This view explains in part the furore over post-menopausal pregnancy that shattered the peace of Christmas 1993. One reason why several European governments viewed the prospect of older women becoming pregnant with

I cannot judge anybody

The following is taken from an article published in *The Guardian*, 5 January 1994.

The 62-year-old Italian woman whose case has re-sparked the controversy over post-menopausal mothers weeps quietly as she explains: 'I chose to have another child in memory of my son Riccardo, who died at the age of 17 in a road traffic accident, to give him a brother or sister, certainly not to substitute him.'

'I want to have a life too, a life with a child, I want to bring him or her up to the same age as Riccardo. The people who judge me have no idea of the pain I suffer inside me.'

Rosanna della Corte, a patient of Roman gynaecologist Severino Antinori, three months pregnant, says: 'If you only knew what darkness there is in this house, without a young boy who filled it with his joy and smile. I desire so much to have another face to caress, to be able to hear somebody call me mother. The love I will give to this baby could not be given by a 20-year-old mother.'

Mrs della Corte, believed to be the oldest woman to become pregnant, has tried to adopt children, but is too old according to Italian law: 'I wanted to help a 10-year-old boy; I searched in many orphanages but every one made fun of me. One day I read in a paper that Professor Antinori had been able to make pregnant a 55-year-old woman and I said to myself, "if she could do it, so could I." The professor treated me with great humanity, made me have all the necessary tests and said to me, "you are perfect, you can do it".'

She became pregnant at the first attempt, but had a miscarriage. 'Now, after seven attempts, I have succeeded,' she says.'I have got plenty of courage.'

Asked if she believes that there is an upper age limit for artificial insemination, and what she would think of, say, a 70-year-old woman being made pregnant, she says: 'I cannot judge anybody. Look, if I still had my son, I wouldn't have tried. I wish I had been a grandmother. Instead, I will be a mother, if I make it to the end of pregnancy. Certainly, I would think that 70 was old, but first I would want to hear her motivations. If I died, the child would be loved by my cousins and nephews as much as I would love him. The whole village of Canino already loves this baby.'

What does she think of the French government, which wants to prevent the artificial insemination of post-menopausal women? 'I think they are wrong, it's not as if the government has to bring up the children. I won't leave this child without providing for it; I will be able to make sure that he or she has a future.'

Mrs della Corte recognizes that she is a privileged person, who is able to obtain medical services that others cannot, and who is able to ensure that her children will be cared for. She recognizes the responsibilities that come with parenthood – as well as the joys – and rejects the proposition that legislation is required which might deny her this opportunity. She also insists that her age does not make her any the less able to honour the responsibilities of parenthood.

alarm was the fear that in time the state itself would be faced with responsibilities for both a dependent child and a dependent parent. Governments would much prefer parents to become dependent only when children are fully adult. Governments everywhere are keen that care responsibilities remain largely with the family.

More generally, there are many different kinds of interpersonal relationships in which the age difference between an older and younger person is measured against the parent–child standard. It is here that there is huge potential for ageism to raise its ugly head. Often, at times of conflict, the awful phrase: 'I'm old enough to be your mother/father . . .' launches a speech that marks a further decline in relations. Alternatively, more satisfactory relationships might be complicated by social responses to such an age difference. Friendships are expected to be intra-generational.

In many cultures the parent–child relationship has a fundamental significance. There are many differences of course, but the essential and common point is that it is a life-long relationship. It is established and formally recorded at the birth of the child, and is normally permanent and indisputable thereafter. The parent has an intimate involvement in and knowledge of the child's birth and development. Both can refer back to this critical phase in the construction of the child's social identity. There is, potentially, an equivalent but reverse situation at the death of the parent, both expecting the child to be involved in caring for the parent during a final illness, in arranging the funeral and in retaining fond memories and an intimate knowledge of family history. And, prior to this, there may be an expectation that the children will look after parents in their old age. Adults often express the view that having children is insurance for their future needs.

Care relations

I consider the relationship between employed care providers and recipients in the next chapter. Here I am more concerned with the provision of what is commonly referred to as informal care. Margaret Forster's novel *Have the Men Had Enough?* provides a graphic account of the changing relationship between a mother, two daughters and Helen, a granddaughter, as the mother's mental health declines. Consider Helen's reaction to her first visit to her grandmother in a geriatric hospital:

Mum told me about the paint, the smell, the locked door. They're as bad as she said but I'm prepared. I'm not prepared for Grandma though. My stomach churns when I see her. She is like a lump, a mess of tripe, all loose and collapsed and floppy. She has a hideous dress on and big fluffy pompommed slippers and half of what she's had for dinner is down her front. I collapse onto a stool beside her. I say, 'Grandma,' and choke. She opens one eye, barely interested enough to look at me.

(Forster 1989: 214–5)

Helen's experience is not exceptional. Most people who have visited a long-stay ward or a nursing home will have been faced with the classic image of senility and, when this is conveyed by someone previously loved as an ordinary lively person, it is all the more shocking. It is at such moments that we are confronted with the harsh reality of the humiliations that threaten the ending of long lives. Our reaction, like Helen's and those of the staff of the hospital, draws upon a long training in ageism, one that values above all else the independence, competence and capacity that is associated with mature adulthood, and which deplores dependence, incompetence and incapacity.

Informal care

Informal care such as that described by Forster became a critical policy issue in the early 1980s (Equal Opportunities Commission 1980). Research at that time revealed something of the pressure that many middle-aged women were under when having to care for their parents. It seemed that the powerful social expectations that the adult child will care for the ailing parent and that women will care for the sick and dependent had, through rapid demographic changes, conspired to force middle-aged women back into their traditional domestic caring roles. This was happening at the very point, ten years or so on from the heady 1960s, when the women's movement seemed to promise so much: when women seemed to be well placed to assume positions of power within society – not just singly but in significant number. Many aspiring women, including those already engaged in the development of the state's care services, found themselves torn between career or political ambitions and a sense of obligation towards their ageing parents. This made their sense of frustration all the more powerful (McIntosh 1979).

A series of research studies articulated and legitimated this sense of outrage (Parker 1990a), and in 1988 the Carers National Association (CNA) was formed. Green (1988) provided the first authoritative national statistics on carers and this demonstrated that there were as many as six million in the UK, over 10 per cent of the population. The political power of the CNA was boosted by this statistic, even though the validity of this has since been questioned (Parker 1990b). What Green's survey also revealed was that far from women providing virtually all the care, they constituted just 60 per cent of carers. Much debate and some further research followed to discover just who the other 40 per cent were (Arber and Gilbert 1989). It was this research which began to focus attention upon the other myth: far from it being adult children who were providing the bulk of informal care to elderly relatives, spouses were shown to be the primary source, many older than the person being cared for:

> Our findings of the extent of care provided by elderly people support the arguments of the few writers who have challenged the stereotype of elderly people as only recipients of care. The attention given to daughters caring for their parents and parents-in-law needs to be complemented by

acknowledging the very substantial volume of care provided by spouses, many of whom are themselves elderly.

(Arber and Ginn 1990: 451)

Morris (1991) has demonstrated how confining some of the early presumptions about informal care for older and disabled people were. She has pointed to the ageism that was rampant alongside disablism in some of the feminist literature. In the repeated expression of concern with the pressures arising from 'dependence', it becomes clear that much of the rhetoric is closely related to the wider moral panic over the 'burden' of an ageing population.

There has been little recognition that both partners in a care relationship are ordinary people subject to comparable ageing experiences, each celebrating a birthday every twelve months. Rather what has developed is a stereotyped image of an 'un-ageing' carer: people who have sought help from care agencies who have then acknowledged their needs. Conversely, the cared-for have acquired an older, passive, dependent and ageing image: a rather anonymous burden threatening the happiness and health of the carer.

As I argued in Chapter 4, matters of age are not just about need, deprivation and powerlessness, and likewise care in later life is not just about the perceived needs of older people. Some wield remarkable power and contribute enormously to the care of younger people, as a surgery receptionist pointed out:

It's the advantage, you see, if you know a family as a whole and you see Granny, you can say, oh yeah, your little grandson hasn't had such and such injection, and you can bet that next week, that child will be in the surgery.

As with the gerontocracies of national governments, the younger generation can become infuriated as its more expert and up-to-date knowledge is over-ruled by the older generation. When grandparents exercise such power over the care of infants and children, it is not just young parents who may find themselves in conflict over standards of childcare. A certain ageism characterizes many of the caring professions, such as midwives, when they have to compete with the providers of folk wisdom:

I mean my mother-in-law used to give my children pop with sugar in it to take the fizz away. Well it used to drive me mental. Dear, dear! And you still see it now, you know, toddlers with bottles of tea with sugar because granny said it's good for them.

Sexual relations

At the age of 80, Plato outlined the defence of a model old man: someone who was able to think positively about his age. Part of this reads as follows:

I was once present when someone was asking the poet Sophocles about sex, and whether he was still able to make love to a woman; to which he replied, 'Don't talk to me about that; I am glad to have left it behind me and escaped from a fierce and frenzied master.' A good reply I thought then, and still do. For in old age you become quite free of feelings of this sort and they leave you in peace; and when your desires lose their intensity and relax, you get what Sophocles was talking about, a release from a lot of mad masters.

(Plato 1975: 62–4)

His people who are on their own

Consider the following comments of an older couple about old age. We begin with the husband, a 71-year-old man who delivers meals on wheels:

> 'What does old age mean to you?'
>
> I'm working with the old, and some you find really confused at an earlier age than say 70 and then someone in their 80s is as good as someone in their 60s. It's how old age finds you in life. It comes along as my mother used to say, old age is allright, but it brings a friend. And that's what the old answer is . . . I'm no telly man. I'd sooner switch it off and get on with doing something. Mind you, I ain't like everybody else, I'm the one out on his own, I reckon. So all you've got to do is look after yourself and enjoy what time you've got. That's all it really comes to.

Now his wife who has a part-time job too – in an optician's office:

> My husband loves his little job and I like mine. We only do a few hours each day. So old age has not approached us really. He's 71 and I'm 68, but we don't go about like old people. We don't want to look old, don't want to be old. My husband comes home every day with some funny story or a sad story about his people who are on their own in their 80s and things like that. And you think to yourself 'ooh I hope I've not got to come to that.' See what I mean. And he'll say, 'well it comes to us all some time.' But we don't think about it. You have to meet it when it comes, don't you. Well I think that.
>
> (Dixon and Gregory 1987: 23)

The husband has a caring relationship with those older people to whom he delivers meals. He refers to them as 'the old' and sets the description 'really confused' against 'as good as'. In part he is fatalistic, accepting that old age may come to him too, but also believing that he is 'one out on his own', one who is looking after himself.

In contrast, his wife is clearer in her mind. She and her husband don't want to go about like old people, they don't want to look old or to be old, and she hopes they don't have to come to be like 'his people'. It seems that she wants both to be included amongst the not-old and to exclude those whom she perceives to be the old – those who are 'on their own in their 80s'.

Plato's rather extraordinary statement makes him seem like an ordinary person, expressing the wild generalizations that characterize many would-be experts. 'In old age you become quite free of feelings of this sort' – on what moral basis is he able to speak of my old age? This is typical of many public comments upon sex and age that have been made over the centuries. Indeed sex appears to be a field of human activity where a welter of suspicion, assertion, delusion and rationalization completely overwhelms the possibility of any empirical reality being revealed. Comfort expresses this view well:

> In the absence of two disabilities – actual disease and the belief that 'the old' are or should be asexual – sexual requirement and sexual capacity are lifelong . . . For some people, the fantasy of the asexual senior which they had when they were younger became a blueprint for their own ageing, a classical case of bewitchment by expectation.
>
> (Comfort 1977: 190)

What people do in private is their own affair of course. Our concern here is with the destructive power of ageism. A well known birthday card depicts a couple, both naked with lined faces and sagging flesh, both smiling and seemingly toothless. He sits naked on the bed while she, still with curlers in her hair, climbs into a 'Miss Sexy Outfit': a rounded, unblemished skin taken straight from its box. The inside message is 'May all your birthday dreams come true.' In my experience, having displayed ageist birthday cards on several training courses and conferences, people react much more to this card than to the more familiar kind of ageist birthday humour. Some people respond with an instant guffaw sometimes followed by a degree of embarrassment, some don't know how to react and look around for guidance and others, rather more critical, look at it and then express their disgust. Although grossly ageist in displaying an image of what is essentially private activity, the card raises a subtle question: is the outfit a mask of the reality of the older body, or is it on the contrary a representation of the younger self that is masked by the body.

There have been a number of serious attempts to raise the question of older people and sexual activity (Brecher 1993). These have sought to challenge the stereotyped image, often conveyed in birthday cards and ageist humour, of a decline in ability not matched by a decline in inclination. The question arises however: is the promotion of the positive image of older people engaging in satisfying sexual activity just as oppressive as the assumption of increasing disinclination? The appearance on the cover of *New Age* in 1979, of a photograph of an older couple kissing each other with some passion, coupled with the challenging caption 'Oh yes, they do!', drew protests from some members of local Age Concern groups. I felt that this reflected not just the traditional discretion of a particular generation, but also a belief founded in personal experience that for some the truth is 'Oh no, they don't!'

It is often said that sex in old age is one of the last great taboos. Schonfield (1982) comments somewhat sarcastically upon the interest in sexual activity in later life: 'It seems to have become a taboo among gerontologists even to question whether 'society' has a taboo for the aged in this domain' (p. 270). It is certainly the case that there is an enormous literature on the subject in the United States, Wharton (1981), for example, lists over one thousand references in his bibliography on sexuality and ageing.

Perhaps it is more accurate to say that it is the image of ordinary sexuality between older people that is the taboo. Imagining one's parents engaged in sexual intercourse is a challenge frequently raised amongst teenagers. It is the sight of the older un-selfconscious naked body and the possible reality of completely private sexual behaviour which challenges so many cherished beliefs about dirty old men and frustrated spinsters. Imagine if you can the typical reaction to the 'Miss Sexy Outfit' birthday card if, instead of climbing into the costume, the woman was simply discarding an ordinary pair of knickers and if, instead of a caricaturing drawing, the image was an ordinary naturalistic photograph.

Nudity

In the last chapter, I suggested that the sight of sagging and wrinkled skin was associated with unseemly hospital work. Featherstone and Hepworth (1993: 312), however, have argued that Cotier (1991) has shown how the ageing body has 'its own particular beauty and appeal'. Certainly Cotier, by photographing many of his subjects in the Gellert Turkish Baths of Budapest, has revealed something of the cool dignity of older people who are used to nakedness, and who have learnt not to feel embarrassed by their ageing bodies. In my view they form a marked contrast with Clark's admirable portraits of senior athletes in California (1986). The introduction to this collection describes her topic as:

> the persistence of physical youthfulness in the elderly – aging with a lighter heart, if you will. Gaze long enough at these old men and women with their sparse grey hair, their wrinkles, their dewlaps, and all at once the anatomical signs of advancing years grow less and less apparent until at last what you see in each is the glowing core of the youth of long ago.
>
> (Clark 1986: ix)

Positive in spirit though it may be, this statement is dedicated to the ideal of youth not age. And what about the naked body? Etta Clark's mother was the only one who posed nude for her:

> She's an accomplished skier and runner . . . she's a superwoman. She was the only one I had nerve enough to ask to pose in the buff . . . She posed nude for me without hesitation (over the objections of my stepfather and my husband). Her advice to me on how to cope with getting older included this: 'Don't wear your glasses because then you won't get a shock when you look in the mirror.'
>
> (Clark 1986: viii, 76)

What this comment demonstrates so clearly is that the people photographed by Clark are living in a society that admires youth, activity and achievement, but which is subject to an inhibited sexuality that objects to nakedness.

Age differences

Age differences are particularly powerful in those public places where new sexual relations are negotiated – clubs, discos, canteens, etc. Firstly there are enormously powerful sanctions against sexual relations across the child/adult boundary. It is clear that these sanctions represent not ageism but a recognition of age difference and of the abuse that potentially results from the power that the adult can have over the child.

In adulthood, there is strong pressure on adults to engage with someone of like age – even a difference of ten years can be viewed disapprovingly. In part this reflects an ideal of settling down and growing older with someone in a similar position in life, liking the same music and so on. Working against these egalitarian tendencies, is the simple fact that, despite this age homophilia, the male is the older partner in the large majority of heterosexual partnerships (Bytheway 1981). The explanation for this is based in the association between age and power and this is significant in the inter-personal politics of gender.

From time to time, the issue of older women and younger men is discussed publicly – the concept of 'the toy boy' has gained a certain notoriety. In the 1990s, the ageist undertones of this theme are being challenged. The targets of Mutual Admiration, a new singles service in California, are 'Sophisticated Attractive Women and Younger Successful Men Who Empower Each Other'.

Age of consent

The following are the comments of David Starkey, chair of Torche, the Tory Campaign for Homosexual Equality.

> I am absolutely indifferent to the age, provided that it's equal. The people who claim that they are seeking to protect the young should really ask why five years in Wormwood Scrubs protects anybody from sexual abuse. Do they regard the fate of a teenage marriage at 16, in which the likelihood of that marriage splitting within two years is 50 per cent, as something from which men need to be protected less than a quick grope in a public lavatory?
>
> Leave the politicians to arrive at some squalid mess which will not save them from action in the European Court. It's overtly discriminatory. Those who wish either to retain 21 [for sexual majority] or only to go down to 18 have got to justify their position, they've got to justify overt inequality in the law, entrenched with the penalties of the criminal law.
>
> The only thing that's needed is rigorous testing of consent. We've got three words, 'age of consent'; the key word is not what everybody seems to be thinking it is, which is age, the key word is *consent*.

(*The Guardian 2*, 14 January 1994: 5)

This brave and clever letter seems to propose that age is not relevant – Starkey is, he says, absolutely indifferent to it. It is consent that is the key. But he clearly favours the retention of 16 as a universal age of consent – thereby protecting the 16-year-old from a doomed marriage. Is this something from which the law currently protects the 15-year-old? Does the libertarian believe that age should be used to limit the legality of marriage? Should one age such as 16 be designated the age when a person acquires total adult status regarding marriage and sexuality in the eyes of the law?

This service was established by two women in their fifties. One commented: 'Older men make you feel less than you are. I put up with that through my youth, it's a cultural thing.' The other: 'Younger men are raised by more liberated women, so you can be equal with them.'

Their argument is that many women are afraid of breaking marriage traditions, and that they live in a society that tells them they will be unattractive and powerless when they get older. The parties that Mutual Admiration organize give them 'freedom to re-invent themselves' (*The Guardian 2*, 5 January 1994: 9). How often, one might ask, will the phrase 'old enough to be your son' be used by their critics?

Abuse

Sex is closely associated with physical abuse. In a local newspaper in Wales, a city councillor claimed that shouts of 'Get your knickers off, granny' were made to pensioners as 1,700 revellers from a Round Table National Sporting Weekend held in a city park, made their way to their cars. This succinctly reflects the sexual violence and ageist aggression that so easily surfaces through an excess of alcohol.

It is the idea of sexual violence by a physically strong person against someone much weaker that fills the ordinary conscience with horror. Imagine the reality of such assaults and the dialogue that might accompany them, the abusive or patronizing sentiments about the generation represented by the victim. It is in such physically threatening situations that the reality and significance of age difference is most apparent. How does society protect the vulnerable? How does it identify them? Age? If so, how can this avoid being oppressively ageist?

Conclusion

In this chapter I have looked at interpersonal relations and how they can be affected by ageism. Essentially what I have argued is that the celebration of birthdays provides an opportunity for age to be revealed, and in certain ways, for the celebrant to be humiliated. But in the one-to-one act of gift-giving, it provides an opportunity for age differences to be registered. Whether it is within family, care or sexual relationships, the older person has a certain authority based upon experience and knowledge of the past, whereas the younger typically claims a greater awareness of contemporary values. The parent–child relationship serves as a certain standard against which age differences are assessed. It is perhaps in regard to sexuality and the power of ageism in determining behaviour and attitudes, that interpersonal relations are most tightly circumscribed by age prejudice, arguably creating a much greater potential for intergenerational conflict.

7

Is it essential?: Ageism and organizations

In this chapter, I want to explore the relationship between the organization and the individual member. By member, I mean any individual who acquires some formal relationship with the organization. There may be several different classes of member: staff, residents, patients, guests, servants, visitors, administrators, owners, and so on. I am particularly interested in two key features: the management of an organization's activities and its regulations regarding admission and discharge. There is a wide range of organizations in which the age of an individual member or prospective member enters into one or both of these features.

Providing organized care

Age differences were discussed in the previous chapter and they are a critical feature of the provision of organized care: normally those who are employed to provide care, whether by the social services, the health service or by voluntary organizations, are subject to retirement policies and those who receive care for the elderly are required to be over retirement age. Despite this, providers are inclined to deny the importance of age difference:

> It's primarily to do with need and the deployment of resources, not age. It's complicated of course and, although we take account of age in allocating services, when we come to the point of delivery, age itself is irrelevant. In particular, I must say the difference between my age and theirs just doesn't come into it.

This is the kind of thing that might be said. Consider now a stunning advertisement that appeared in the papers in 1993. The text read as follows:

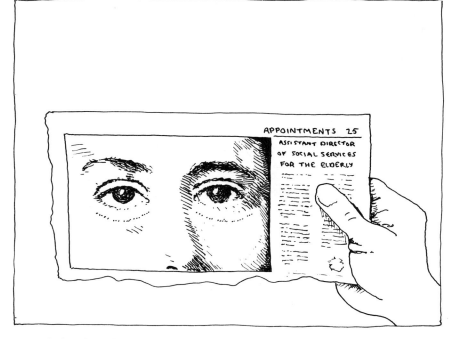

Apply for this job because . . . one day you'll be old too.

Assistant Director of Social Services for the Elderly.
It's a frightening thought.

But here's your chance to make it less of a worry for Bradford's 70,000 elderly residents. (And for yourself too if you stay with us long enough, which we suspect you might because both the area and the job have a lot to offer).

. . .

After all, whoever we are, we'll all be old one day.

(*The Guardian*, 20 May 1992)

The copy-writer and the designer have attempted to break through ageist barriers to working with older people by appealing to the reader's self-interest. To the face of a female prospective applicant, the caption 'Apply for this job because . . . one day you'll be old too' doubles up as the prospective bags under the presently youthful eyes. The advertisement endeavours to bring home to potential candidates the truth of their own personal futures. It constructs an image of the successful candidate as someone not yet old, who is frightened by the thought that one day she will be, but someone who can help to reduce the worries of those already elderly and thereby take positive steps to making her own old age more bearable.

Through the formal organization of care provision, age is *made* significant and relevant to the relationship between the service provider and the service receiver at *every* level – from the statutes, through the appointment of officers (in response to advertisements such as the above), the allocation of resources, the training systems, the specialization of professional interests, the contract of employment and retirement age, the allocation of cases, through to the knock on the door and personal introductions, to the shaking of hands, the helping into ambulances, the body on the stretcher, and the intimacy of looking into eyes.

Providers and recipients

Most organizations providing care make a clear distinction between providers and recipients: a service is provided and received. This asymmetrical interpersonal relationship is dominant in the structuring and management of activities. Outside the immediate context of the service being delivered the lives of the provider and recipient are irrelevant: in the planning of nursing services, for example, what the nurse has to offer is no more (and no less) than what nursing has to offer. In the course of a typical day, the nurse may provide nursing care to several recipients but the several are no more (and no less) than the recipient several times over. Similarly, one particular recipient may receive care from several nurses, one succeeding another because of illness, holidays, resignations, promotion and so on, but again the service provided to the recipient remains unchanged: it is being provided by the nurse. In regard to services for the elderly, the age constraints imposed by management ensure that the provider is very much the younger – as the advertisement for the Assistant Director of Social Services demonstrates.

No ball games

The following is an account provided by a young male social worker of a minor crisis on a London housing estate.

> We get at cross purposes sometimes in the team, particularly with the youth workers. Quite naturally they favour their clients and we favour ours. There was an instance a few months ago when we nearly came to blows: there was a meeting here in this building attended by about 40 people, and a right riot it nearly was. We – myself and my co-worker Jean – had had a lot of complaints from elderly people living in Providence in the ground-floor flats at Preston and Lancaster; there were complaints about kids playing football on the small patch of grass in between, and kicking footballs into their very tiny gardens or as happened on one occasion through somebody's bedroom window. So without really sitting down and thinking out the situation, we had a notice made and erected on that particular piece of grass saying 'No Ball Games'. The youth workers were incensed at what they considered to be a high-handed action on our part and removed the notice. One of our elderly volunteers immediately informed us that it had been taken away 'by the kids' as he thought. So we put up another one and asked the local police to keep an eye on it, as well as two of the senior citizens who could see it

---

from their window and who had telephones. The net result of that was that when the two youth workers who were under the impression the notice had been put up by the council arrived and started to pull up the pole the notice was on and take it away again, a police car was there in two minutes and they were arrested and told they were going to be charged with criminal damage. The police I think were under the impression too that the notice was council property.

It took dozens of phone calls and memos to get it all sorted out. The police were very displeased and threatened us with prosecution for erecting the notice on GLC land in the first place, the youth workers were more convinced than ever that we were a toffee-nosed lot who threw our weight around, and there was general confusion and bad feeling.

It was eventually resolved as it should have been in the first place by calling all the interested parties together, including some of the boys who played football there. And with everyone sitting down round a table to solve the problem, it proved very simple. It was the boys themselves who suggested they should rearrange the lie of their football pitch so there was no danger of the ball going anywhere near the old people's windows.

(Parker 1983: 292–3)

Community work is a form of advocacy which can work well in representing the interests of deprived or vulnerable people who have difficulty in articulating their feelings or needs. It seems more contentious when workers begin to represent the conflicting sections of the community. Whatever else, it seems absurdly ageist to have those working with young people set against those working with elderly people.

Meeting needs

Much of the planning and training for the delivery of services is based upon a standard model of service provision. Doctors, for example, receive a comprehensive training in the diagnosis and treatment of medical conditions. We expect them to provide effective treatment when we are ill. Many disciplines are developing agreed professional standards, and quality assurance is a growing concern in the management of practice. One of the consequences of this is the standardization of needs. Sidell, for example, quotes an older woman:

He takes a blood test, and apparently in the blood test it tells him whether . . . something to do with the white and black blood cells, whether they sink or not, and it's how they sink is how bad this complaint is. So every time I go, he just says, 'How are you? Oh, you're all right. I think you'd better have another blood test.' So I've had a blood test every time I've gone, and they are going by the blood test and nothing else. And you can't say to him about your back because he's not interested in that, he won't want to know anything else except treating me for this complaint which he says I had, this virus.

(Sidell 1993: 182)

It can be claimed, of course, that Sidell's example is untypical, a case of bad practice, but there is growing evidence that services are becoming more routinized and modularized in this way. When managers talk of care becoming more individualized with care packages being tailored to meet individual need, what is actually on offer are packages variously made up of standardized elements. And the more this becomes dependent upon a team approach to providing care, the more important it is that team leaders are reassured that the various elements of a package meet agreed standards.

Gray and Willcock provide a vivid example of how older people can be seriously threatened by failures in their multi-provider care systems – systems over which they have no control or responsibility:

> Mrs S. is 82 and lives in a block of sheltered flats. One morning she was observed by a neighbour walking to the shops at 7.30 a.m., one-and-a-half hours before they opened. The neighbour took her by the arm and led her back to her flat. Ten minutes later the same neighbour saw her walking to the shops once more and took her back to her flat a second time. This time, Mrs S. became disturbed; the GP was called; he prescribed a tranquillizer, and she slept all day. At 5.30 p.m. she walked to the common room of the block of flats to play bingo, which did not start until 7.30 p.m. She was taken back to her flat by one resident, another came in to make her a cup of tea, a third called the warden, who rang the GP again and contacted her son. At this point the woman became very disturbed, claiming that people were trying to kill her, and the GP said he would ask for a second opinion from a consultant psychiatrist. It was then discovered that her son had turned her clock *back* an hour instead of turning it *forward* the previous evening which had been the spring equinox.
>
> (Gray and Willcock 1981: 30–1)

There can be little doubt that Mrs S. was being attended to by caring people who were acting as a well-coordinated team. Many would think her lucky to have such support. But her life was put in serious danger because the team was drawing upon a stereotyped model of old age, and in particular an excessive willingness to diagnose dementia. They were jumping to conclusions rather than giving attention to what Mrs S. had to say and to simple explanations for the only problem that required explanation: that of getting the time wrong.

Containing costs

Once the needs of an individual are identified satisfactorily, the services provided and a routine established, there often follows a crisis over cost. Fixed annual budgets often hinder responses to unexpected crises and it is often existing long-term commitments that then suffer. This is well illustrated

The only sound

It is half past eleven in an old people's home. The morning drinks have been taken and the cups collected. In a small lounge with fire doors at each end, ten old ladies are sitting quietly along two walls. Some are staring ahead of them and some appear to be dozing. Through one of the fire doors comes a member of staff carrying a small suitcase. Behind her is a thin old man holding his hat in front of him with both hands. In the room she turns, asks him to sit in a vacant chair, places the suitcase in front of him, and goes out through the other door. The old man is dressed in a dark suit with a white shirt, dark tie, and polished black shoes. The suit is cut in a very old style and has been carefully pressed which makes him look as though he is on his way to a Sunday service or a funeral. He holds the hat very tightly in his lap and his hands are shaking. Some of the old ladies glance at him and then look away. After several minutes of silence another staff member comes in carrying a piece of paper and a pen, reads an address to him, and asks if that is the correct address of his next of kin. He clears his throat and says it is. After she has gone, he sits forward stiffly in the chair, gazing at the floor in front of his suitcases. Ten minutes elapse. The first member of staff returns with a cup of tea and asks if he would like sugar. He shakes his head. She hands him the cup of tea and departs again. As he sits holding his hat and the cup, the shaking of his hand makes the cup rattle loudly. It is the only sound. He sips quickly at the tea. Before he can finish, the staff member returns again, says that his room is ready, picks up his suitcase and goes through the door holding it open for him. He rises quickly to his feet, holding his hat and half-finished cup of tea and looks around. There are no tables in the room and he balances the cup on a window ledge behind the seat, before hurrying out of the room. The old ladies who have looked up at his departure return their gaze to the walls and floor.

(Godlove *et al.* 1982: 56–7)

Like Tower Hospital studied by Henry (page 29), this account illustrates something of the imbalance of power in the relationship between provider and recipient in an institutional setting, and of the experience of being admitted as a recipient of the service.

by a discussion between two receptionists regarding the availability of appliances for older people:

DR: I think with the elderly people, for appliances now, I think they're tending to run out of appliances at the moment . . . So we are finding difficulty in getting them.

MR: They rang about a fortnight ago from the services, didn't they? And said that they'd run out of bath chairs, they'd only hand-rails available at the moment.

DR: And when you're old you need it.

MR: Well that's it. It's awkward then to tell somebody that, you know, you do need a bath chair but you can't have one. (laugh)

They then moved on to discuss the need for ambulance escorts:

MR: It's awkward with the escorts, because when you book an ambulance they say: 'Is it medically essential for an escort?', but if you've got an elderly person who's going down to the hospital . . .

DR: And they don't know where they're going . . .

MR: You know, they don't know where they're going, they get confused. Obviously they want to take an escort.

MR: And like a lot of the old people, where they're confused, they need somebody really, don't they, to be with them.

DR: They say, you know, the doctor has to say . . .

MR: It might not be medically essential but, you know, they might be fit enough to walk in and around the hospital, but it's just like having company and somebody to show them where to go in.

DR: Now they actually say, 'Has the doctor said that they need an escort?'

MR: And then when you tend to ask the people: 'Is, you know, is it essential?', they get, well, it's not offended but they get upset, and they say 'Well, you know, I can walk but I want somebody with me.' It's awful, you know, it's awful awkward then.

The consequences of growing pressure towards these kinds of rationing were made clearly apparent in a letter to *The Guardian* commenting on the prosecution of Dr Nigel Cox following the death of Mrs Boyes:

Through my work as a union official I am in touch with an experiment in one London borough which is replacing the home help services with a 'flying squad' of cleaners. One case drawn to the council's attention involves a housebound woman in her eighties who looked to her home help of five years for help of every imaginable sort. She cried profusely over her withdrawal. The first she knew about it was last Monday morning when nobody turned up. She had to struggle to an outside toilet to empty her commode – for the first time since the previous Friday. Another concerned a 98-year-old woman, blind and clinging to life with a pacemaker. She too has lost her home help – upon whom she was intensely dependent both for practical and emotional support. Just how natural and dignified a death do such people face . . . Mrs Boyes' wish to die was motivated only by natural pain. A whole generation may soon be wishing it were dead because of state sponsored cruelty and deprivation. This is the problem we face. Dr Cox's punishment is a hypocritical red herring.

(*The Guardian*, 29 September 1992: 16)

It is easy to see in these accounts evidence of a cruel form of ageism. The older person who asks for help, is assessed professionally, then offered and receives appropriate services, becomes dependent upon them, and then, not because of any recovery or change in need, is denied these services because, it is claimed, 'we' can no longer afford them.

Payments

The present Government, in its efforts to reduce the costs of care for older people, has also been increasing the payments being asked of recipients and their families. Jill Pitkeathley, Director of the Carers National Association, has commented about the plight of some owner occupiers:

> These changes are happening by stealth with no public debate. Every day carers contact us for whom it comes as a total surprise that owner occupation is being used in this way. People's expectation is still that if they have cared for someone as long as they possibly can, there will be good care available free when they can no longer cope.
>
> (*The Guardian*, 5 August 1993: 2)

When families face these kinds of costs, they are increasingly taking advantage of one of the few care services that is still freely available: admission to hospital care through emergency and casualty departments. In July 1993, the British Medical Association decided to investigate 'granny-dumping'. Increasingly, hospitals are unable to discharge older patients from acute NHS wards because there is nowhere for them to go. Families insist that they are unable to provide the care or to meet the costs of alternative care. A spokesperson for the BMA commented:

> The burden is falling increasingly on the very people who have funded the welfare state all their lives and thought it would provide for their basic needs from cradle to grave. Now they face the prospect of having their homes and pensions sequestered to pay for long-term care.
>
> (*The Independent*, 1 July 1993: 6)

It is in this way that governmental panic over the 'burden' of the ageing population is being passed down on to the recipients of services and their families. The connection between the perception of older people as a burden and the allocation of resources was made particularly clear in a letter to the *New Statesman and Society*. It began by arguing that:

> if it were not for a poorly built and inhospitable environment older people would be able to manage fairly well, in other words we manufacture their dependence.

The correspondent goes on to challenge the 'insulting' concept of the blocked bed:

> The fact that they do need a bed for longer, and it is therefore not available for another patient, is really the fault of the manager and planners for failing to provide adequate beds to service the local communities in line with the population needs.
>
> (*New Statesman and Society*, 23 March 1993: 6)

A poorly built and inhospitable environment
Photograph: Brenda Price, Format

In short, governmental panic over public expenditure has denied older people the sense of security in their later life for which they have been paying for many years – the national insurance system has failed.

Gerontology

Gerontology is an academic discipline and, like other disciplines and occupations, individuals identify with it. In 1971 the British Society of Gerontology was established with the purpose of providing opportunities for gerontologists in Britain to gather and collaborate in the development of the discipline.

During the 1970s, as we noted in Chapter 3 (pages 31 and 41), both the Gray Panthers and Levin and Levin (1980) pointed to the ageism of American gerontology. More generally, Townsend (1986) has argued that a number of academic and scientific theories have shaped policies regarding the needs of the elderly. In particular he identifies a body of thought about ageing which he refers to as 'acquiescent functionalism', which 'legitimates ageism in practice in contemporary society'. It:

> attributes the causes of most of the problems of old people to the natural consequence of physical decrescence and mental inflexibility or to the failures of individual adjustment to ageing and retirement, instead of to contemporary developments of the state, the economy and social inequality.
>
> (Townsend 1986: 19)

In writing this book it has been tempting to adopt this heretical view: to argue that gerontology is essentially ageist. Certainly the participation of older people in British gerontology has been unacceptably low, and little has been done to challenge the continuing tendency of those agencies that fund gerontological research to invest in the appointment of new graduates to short-term research contracts. As a consequence, much gerontological research is undertaken by younger people with a degree in some discipline other than gerontology. Stimulating though much of their work is, their publications have tended to enhance the sense of their subjects being of a different world, a different age. In addition to this bias in recruitment into the discipline, many of the basic British texts on gerontology fail to give the concept of ageism the critical attention it deserves.

In September 1993 I attended the annual conference of the Society. The theme was The Experiences of Older People – Solidarity across the Generations. In preparing an account of the conference for the BSG's journal *Generations Review*, I identified a heightened consciousness of two issues which distinguished it from previous conferences: the role and impact of the researcher, and the ages of the participants at the conference. Both relate to the potential impact of ageism upon the Society.

I attended the presentations of seven papers and it was clear from these that the seven researchers were actively participating in real-life situations in which age was of considerable importance. Two papers in particular clearly demonstrated that, in an ageist world, gerontology depends heavily upon the researcher who maintains a careful record of what is observed as well as of what is said or written:

- Geraldine Lee-Treweek reported on what she had observed in nursing home bedrooms, as auxiliary care workers 'ordered' patients into a presentable condition for the more public areas of the home. She described how she grew sick (i) of patients' questions going unanswered or unlistened-to (for example: 'What's the weather like?' 'In a minute'); (ii) of patients being teased and verbally abused ('Stop playing the dying duck!'); and (iii) of writing out her field notes since the routines were always the same. Within this taxing and demoralizing environment, she found her own values were constantly tested by the brutality of the regime.
- Second, a participant who should remain anonymous provided a vivid account of how, through the implementation of new policies on payments for home help services, older clients were being forced into debt (confirming the observations of the Carers National Association – see page 95 above). The fact that her job in the local authority was threatened by her participation in the conference brought home to us how the welfare of researchers in gerontology is sometimes threatened by ageist institutions.

All seven papers, however, were offered by younger people employed, I suspect, by agencies that had formal age-specific retirement policies. Their fieldwork, with one exception, drew upon the lives and thoughts of people over pensionable age. Discussions of these kinds of research all too often reduce to the question of: 'What have we learnt about these older people?'

Clumped together

The organizers of the conference had selected the theme 'the experiences of older people' and, in the final plenary session, a panel of five older gerontologists took the platform. All five addresses were particularly interesting, but Tilda Goldberg began hers by saying that she would have preferred the contributions of older people to have been peppered throughout the conference programme, and not clumped together for the last session. Her criticism appeared to be a thinly veiled objection to this last session symbolizing the ageism of the wider society. In my report I commented as follows:

> Although the us/them divide in this instance represents the distinction between presenters and audience, their position – selected on grounds of age and 'clumped together' on the platform – turned them into representatives of 'the elderly', by implication, the 'proper' subject of 'our' studies. In this way, the session reinforced the belief that older people are different and separable; that we are 'ageless' and they are 'ageful'.
>
> (Bytheway 1993b: 20)

For a brief period, the Society was divided between them, the older gerontologists on the stage, and we, the audience hearing what they had to say.

Normally, age is not a criterion for sorting out the membership or participation in the conference. This event was exceptional and revealing.

Equal opportunities

Early in 1993, I obtained details of a vacant post in a British university. These were accompanied by a statement of its Equal Opportunities Policy:

> The University . . . confirms its commitment to a comprehensive policy of equal opportunities in employment and for students in which individuals are selected and treated on the basis of their relevant merits and abilities and are given equal opportunities within the University. The aim of the policy is to ensure that no job applicant or employee, prospective student or student, should receive less favourable treatment on any grounds which are relevant to good employment practice for staff or to academic ability and attainment for students. The University is committed to a programme of action to make the policy fully effective.

This lengthy statement makes no reference to specific grounds upon which treatment might be less favourable. However, accompanying the details there was an Equal Opportunities Policy Form to be completed by prospective applicants. In the preamble it is explained that information is required on 'key characteristics which relate to equal opportunities in employment', and that the Policy is intended to ensure that there be no discrimination on the grounds of 'sex, colour, race, marital/family status or disability'.

There followed five questions relating to these five characteristics. There was, however, no request for information about age. Even the standardized application form for the vacant post did not request age or date of birth, and so it began to appear that age was of no relevance or interest, and incidentally that the University would be in no position to assess the relationship of applicants to its compulsory retirement and pension policies. However, at the very bottom of the Equal Opportunities Form, following concluding thanks and confirmation that the information would only be used for monitoring purposes, there was a request for the applicant's date of birth. It is not at all clear from this (a) whether or not age is part of the Equal Opportunities Policy, (b) if so, whether it will be monitored using this record of birth date, and (c) why it was not incorporated into the main body of the Form.

Consider a hypothetical male applicant who – in 1994 – enters 1912 as his date of birth at the bottom of this Form. It seems reasonably certain that if his application is otherwise attractive then some action would follow. It may be thought, for example, that he has made a simple error. If so, it is possible that the personnel office would then check the application form. Although, not including date of birth or age, the form might reveal, for example, that the applicant had obtained a degree in 1935 and that his work history began in the following year. This would suggest that the date of birth is correct and that the applicant is indeed 82 years of age. On the other hand, it may be that the application form reveals that he obtained his first degree in 1975. If so, it might still be possible that he had been a mature student aged 63 years upon graduation. After all, universities are more than happy to admit mature students.

If it is felt that the applicant should be short-listed, and if the 1912 is the only indication that the applicant might be 82 years of age, the personnel department will be concerned. There is a serious danger that the university will be funding the interview expenses of someone who, on grounds of age alone, would not be eligible for appointment under 'the general conditions applicable to the post' (a clause included in the further details). Does the personnel officer write to the applicant? Does he or she discuss the matter with those who will be preparing the shortlist? How is the potential embarrassment of age being requested and revealed, to be managed? What are the implications of the Equal Opportunities Policy for this problem? All these questions relate to good employment practice regarding age. As employers, we should ask ourselves if we are concerned to know the age of prospective applicants and, if so, why. And, as applicants, are we prepared to declare our age in applying for a vacant post and, if so, under what conditions?

Ageing workforce

One reason why the university might be interested in the age of applicants is that, with the decline of state investment in higher education over the last decade or so, there has been an increasing average age of lecturers in universities. A few years ago, a modest national recruitment programme was directed specifically at the appointment of young lecturers. They were given the ageist title: 'new blood' appointments.

More recently the Association of University Teachers expressed concern over the increasing numbers of lecturers aged 50 or more, and it was promptly admonished by a number of its members. The following is one of the letters published in its newsletter:

> I really thought that ageism, like sexism, was banned by AUT. First you told us (reassuringly, if ungrammatically) that one in three of us were over 50, and then you spoiled it with 'even worse' news. What's bad about our maturity and experience? One in three of us was proud of our seniority (and – dare I say it? – our old-fashioned command of English) until you condemned us as an 'ageing academic workforce'. I'm already nine years over the limit, and annually getting even worse, it seems. I'll ponder this defect over a glass of ageing port and try hard to see it your way.
>
> (*Update*, 27 January 1994: 4)

Where, therefore, does higher education stand on the question of age and equal opportunities?

Retirement

In the discussion of care-providing organizations at the beginning of this chapter, I focused upon the relationship between provider and recipient. In this section I want to look at the relationship between the employing organization and the employee in regard to the latter's retirement. We could be talking about a Care Assistant and the local authority that employs her.

Employment involves a legal contract which ensures that the employee gives time to the employer on a regular, normally daily, basis. Because of this time element, employment is critical to the establishment of social status.

'What do you do?'

'I'm a Care Assistant.'

An extraordinary answer but for the implication that she spends so many hours a day, so many days a week, so many weeks a year, providing care. Having a job is important to her not just because it provides her with activities that keep her occupied during the day, week and year, but an answer to the question of what she does. It also provides her with what, for much of her life, will be her primary means of gaining an income in her own name.

At a certain age, presently 60 for women and 65 for men in the UK (but not for much longer), a person becomes eligible for a state pension. Twenty years ago the relative value of this was greater than it is now. But tied to it was the 'earnings rule', as a result of which any income subsequently gained through employment was followed by an appropriate deduction from the state pension. This meant that pensionable age was almost always retirement age. The two went together. More recently the relative value of the state pension has declined, occupational and personal pensions have expanded, and the earnings rule has been removed. The consequence of this has been to relax the links between pension, retirement and age (Laczko and Phillipson 1991). Many people who are drawing a pension, for example, also have an income from employment. Conversely many older unemployed workers – people out of work but under pensionable age – think of themselves as retired because they have no expectation of gaining further paid employment (Bytheway 1987).

The critical issue to be addressed is: in what ways is the age of the individual worker taken into account in planning an exit from employment. I would argue that there are three ways in which age, and thereby ageism, affects the retirement process. The first is the effect of cultural ageism upon expectations of the older worker. The second is the impact of government legislation and, in particular, the regulation of state pensionable age. And the third is the way the employing organization itself imposes age limits upon continued employment. It is to the last of these that I now want to turn.

Redundancy

In the wake of the twelve-week 1980 national steel strike, the British Steel Corporation announced 'Slimline', a major redundancy scheme for the Abbey works in Port Talbot in South Wales. It proposed that about 5,000 men be made redundant (Fevre 1989). There was no offer of work adjustments to protect older workers who stayed on after Slimline (although this had happened in the past). Older workers realized that continuation implied even greater physical demands being placed upon those remaining in a slimmed-down workforce. What Slimline offered the worker aged 55 or more were three significant carrots: a single payment, varying considerably but on average of the order of one to two years' wages, the Readaptation Benefit (popularly known as 'make-up money') bringing income up to 90 per cent of previous earnings in

Eighty-year-old Marjorie Cooper in the sixth form at her local school, in Pontypool, studying for A levels
Photograph: Mo Wilson

the first year after redundancy and then 80 per cent in the second year, and a works pension for the remainder of their lives. Two features of Slimline made it clear that older workers were being encouraged to leave not just the employment of the Corporation but also the local labour market. The make-up money was paid automatically – and, as a result (as had been the case of the earnings rule for state pensioners), there would be no financial gain through obtaining employment during the first two years. In contrast, those made redundant under the age of 55 would only receive make-up money when they obtained employment – a strong incentive to find work, any work. Second, older workers were immediately eligible for the works pension, whereas those under 55 had to wait until they reached state pensionable age before receiving it – unless they had a disability. These contrasts created a certain moral obligation on older workers not to seek work – to do so, it was argued, would deprive younger unemployed men to whom work would bring greater financial advantage (Bytheway 1986).

So, in Port Talbot in the early 1980s, the major local employer was actively managing the composition of the local labour market through age regulations. There can be little doubt that the training centre which sought to deny the 58-year-old the chance to become a brickie (pages 3–4) knew of this and shared the belief that older workers should make way for younger men. Another man, in his early sixties, had obtained seasonal work in Porthcawl, a holiday resort, during the first three years of redundancy. But in 1984, in the queue once again for the same work, he made way deferring to the needs of a

Going back to school

The following comes from an interview with a resident of the same estate that survived the football crisis (page 90–1 above). He lives alone and describes himself as a 'senior unretired citizen':

A few years ago, about the week after my seventieth birthday I think it was, I went to the Education Department people and asked them if I could go to school. 'Yes', they said. 'Of course you can, here's the list of all the night classes we've got.' I said I didn't want night classes. I wanted proper school; there were a lot of things I'd like to know a bit about to begin with, and then go on further with one or two I fancied to follow up. 'Well go to the library', they said. 'They've got books there about every subject you could think of, have a good look round and see what takes your fancy.' I said I thought going to the library was all right, but you needed somebody to guide you with study, and anyway I didn't want to read a big book about something to find out whether I was going to be interested in it or not. Then they said well what sorts of subjects did I have in mind; I said that was the whole idea, I couldn't tell until I knew what there was. Geography, history, French, sums, which I think they call 'number' now, plants and animals and stars and English and so on – what I wanted was to go to an ordinary school where I could learn first of all what there was to learn. I wanted to do it full time, all day each day – proper school. No they said, they were very sorry but they didn't have anywhere like that. I said, 'Yes you do'. I said, 'There's a school over the road there. Let me go there like the children do, and be given homework and have my books marked and everything. Only I'd have to be excused the PT in the gymnasium.' First of all they laughed. But I said, 'Look I'm serious.' When they realized I was, they thought I must be mental. They said I couldn't do it, it wasn't allowed. So that was that, and I was very disappointed about it.

(Parker 1983: 130)

This is a classic tale of stereotyped expectations being challenged. The moral is that anyone who thinks they have a right to schooling regardless of age must be 'mental'.

younger man. He continued, however, to walk around town looking for 'hobbles' (unofficial paid work) such as digging gardens. Another man had spent much of his life as a draper in Port Talbot. He had been in the steelworks for only nine years and so was offered only a small pension. He had heavy expenses to meet as a result of purchasing a faulty council house but could not return to his former trade or obtain alternative work. The financial security of these men had been substantially reduced by the use of age by the Steel Corporation in regulating the local labour market.

Many of the older redundant workers did well out of the deal – those who had served in the steelworks for many years, who had risen to senior positions and who were near to retirement age. But even they did not like the way in which their exit from working life was managed. They had expected the usual modest retirement ceremony on their 65th birthday. They had seen this happen so often and had passed on their best wishes to many of their older workmates who had retired. Instead they felt they had been bundled out en masse, with little consideration for their feelings: redundancy had reduced their retirement to a matter of money and many felt guilty that they had been 'bought off'.

When I interviewed them in 1984/85, South Wales was in the throes of the miners' strike. Many had started out as miners, moving to the steelworks in the 1960s and 1970s when their mine had been closed. They viewed with dismay the way in which the miners' employer, the National Coal Board, backed by the government, was seeking to sever the contract they had with thousands of employees.

Any organization that enters into legal, social and moral contracts with individuals has to consider carefully the ways in which it manages the processes of admitting and discharging them. When age is a factor in admission or when the contract extends over many years, then it is almost inevitable that the organization will be suspect to ageist inclinations. Whether it is hospitals taking on new staff or handling patients, commercial firms doing business with customers, colleges appointing staff and admitting students, airlines allocating seats, or newspapers running human interest stories, agents of such organizations are expected to take account of the ages of the individuals involved. How might they avoid being ageist? This is the question that is to be addressed in the third part of this book.

Conclusion

It is all too easy first to associate ageism with individual attitudes, and to overlook the contribution of organizations and other structural aspects of society, and then, in restoring the balance, to focus upon ageism at the macro-level of national statistics and government policies: the structured dependency, for example, that emerges from pension policies and health and welfare legislation. What I have attempted in this chapter is to point to examples of ageism in the neglected middle area: to demonstrate how, whether it is providing care, organizing academic life or producing steel, the structuring of the organization and its activities, the development of standards and the impact of budgetary controls, all contribute to the creation of relationships in which ageism can flourish. Similarly, the staffing policies, recruitment procedures, career structures and retirement programmes, in controlling the flow of people through an organization, can impose an ageist culture upon its daily life and activities.

PART III

Rethinking ageism

In the final two chapters, I attempt to meet the objective of this series of books: in this case to rethink ageism. In so doing, I will be referring back to the material that has gone before.

Most of those who have written about ageism have tended to presume that it exists and that, as a concept, it is self-explanatory. Some, however, think of ageism primarily as age discrimination in employment practices and that it mainly affects people in their forties, fifties and sixties – they would be surprised if it were to be suggested that exactly the same phenomenon affected the lives of people in their nineties. Others think of ageism as the pressure to maintain a youthful appearance, something they abandon, somewhat ostentatiously perhaps, in their thirties – while still sustaining a fashionable appearance. Others, typically the newly retired, think of ageism primarily as the impoverishment of pensioners and, in their political battles to raise the value of the state pension, they may overlook other forms of impoverishment that less active older people suffer. In these ways, it is easy to think of ageism in the narrow context of one aspect of age, one that is associated with a comparatively limited range of ages, so that once again – in the battle against ageism of all things – various groups of older people come to be excluded.

8

Theories of age

Rethinking ageism should begin with a review of how age is theorized. We all have theories about the ageing process: ways of explaining, understanding and anticipating what is to come and how older people come to be how they are. We need theory to be able to talk about something so intangible as ageing.

Many theories have become institutionalized in educational and training curricula on the basis of knowledge obtained through scientific enquiry. Others have been devised as people in the course of everyday life have struggled to understand and articulate the signs of ageing around them. It might be argued that theories can only come out of systematic and scientific study, that they have to be published and that they have to receive a certain acceptance before they can be called *theory*. In contrast, Gubrium and Wallace offer the following justification for studying popular theory:

> This paper concerns how to evaluate the differences by moving beyond the bounds of formal assessment to ask, *in general*, who theorises age? The emphasis is meant to suggest that not just professional social gerontologists theorise age: we all do to the extent that we set about the task of attempting to understand the whys and wherefores of growing old. It is argued that when the proprietory bounds of gerontological theorising are set aside, striking parallels can be found between the theorising of ordinary men and women concerned with ageing and their more celebrated gerontological peers.
>
> (Gubrium and Wallace 1990: 132)

From an analysis of evidence of ordinary theorizing obtained through ethnographic fieldwork, they conclude:

> When we suspend the natural attitude and allow the ordinary theoretical activity of the aged and others to become visible, a whole world of

reasoning about the meaning of growing old, becoming frail and caregiving comes forth. We find that theory is not something exclusively engaged in by scientists. Rather, there seem to be two existing worlds of theory in human experience, one engaged by those who live the experiences under consideration, and one organised by those who make it their professional business systematically to examine experience. To the extent we all attend to experience and attempt to understand it or come to terms with its varied conditions, we all theorise age. To privilege scientific theorising simply on the basis of its professional status makes scientistic what otherwise would be firm recognition of the theoretical activity of ordinary men and women, along with the opportunity to refocus social gerontology from behaviours to meanings embedded in ordinary discourse.

(Gubrium and Wallace 1990: 147)

Rather obliquely, this is proposing that when gerontology becomes scientistic and behaviouristic it also becomes ageist.

Theorizing as an activity

I want to contrast now two extreme examples of theorizing. In Bytheway (1993a), I presented evidence from an analysis of the published writings of Mary Berenson. She theorized on the basis of her own experience of age.

Experiential theorizing

She was born in 1864 in Philadelphia. In 1900 she married Bernard Berenson. Both were closely involved in the world of art in the first half of this century. She constantly wrote letters to her family and friends. Many of her comments on the processes and patterns of change reflect her theories of ageing. A letter written in 1907 to her daughters (by a previous marriage) is a good example. Bernard had told her he was at a great crisis:

> I said 'The truth is that THIS time you have really and truly come to the end of your mental energy. All is over. You will never write or think again. Your brain is already attacked with fatty degeneration and you are doomed to pass a dull, idle unthinking existence. Of course these symptoms, in the past, have come about as regularly as the trees shed their leaves, about once a year, but THIS time it is of course utterly different; this time it really is all over!' He could not deny that I had hit off his mysterious complaint pretty well. I have noticed that he always feels like that a few months before he sets to work on something new . . . Are we all as unconscious as that, taking our habitual peculiarities with such gravity?
> (Strachey and Samuels 1983: 137–8)

What Mary put to Bernard is a model of ageing: he was suffering from fatty degeneration in the brain and was doomed to an idle existence. She had come to recognize how periodically he held this distinctly negative model of his ageing. On this occasion he believed that she had understood that this time it was different: it was indeed all over. The idea of irreversibility is a critical element in theorizing age.

I identified eight models of age in her letters and diaries. The first, the *developmental* model, is the basis of being 'more and more grown up', of 'filling gaps' and 'learning new tricks'. In her final years, her memory 'grows and grows'. A second model is that of the *status quo*. It lies behind words such as 'constantly', 'always', 'never' and 'same'. The idea of the mask, of an unageing self detached from an ageing body, is apparent in phrases such as 'a life being led', 'somehow buried in flesh' and 'an old woman's existence'. Similar to this is the third model: ageing as *routine*. Ageing is the experience of events happening routinely: 'regular symptoms', 'incessant letters', 'habitual peculiarities' and, as in the above 'as regularly as the trees shed their leaves'.

Fourth, there is the *stages* model. As one stage succeeds another, you accept that things will be 'utterly different'. Middle age is seen as an inevitable muddling of places and names, and you anticipate the pleasures that life 'stores up for your old age'. With illness, Mary decided to 'settle down to become an invalid'. Fifth, there is negative change, the *decline* model. This underlies the 1907 model of Bernard's ageing. The phrase 'more and more' is used to represent both growth and decline. Part of the concept of decline entails loss and one of Mary's doctors offered some strikingly ageist comment on this. When she visited him:

> I couldn't scrape up any symptoms, except perhaps a bit of old-age laziness, and he rather laughed at me. However he said that fat old ladies did tend to lose their grip, and that he could help them by his system of feeding the glands by means of injections of (as I understand) gland extract.
>
> (Strachey and Samuels 1983: 264)

Sixth, we have the model of *extremes*. It is represented by extremes of experience: 'you can't think how seriously ill I've been' (in 1918) and 'never enjoyed myself so much', and also of age: 'so old', a 'stretch of years as great as . . .'. Seventh, there is age the *adversary*. Consider her comments on Bernard's crises: his brain was 'attacked' and he was 'doomed' and, in 1922, she wrote 'Anno Domini was too much for him'. A short sentence 'Life took its course', written in 1927, raises the crucial question of whether Mary ever felt she could resist the changes that were happening in her life. She only seemed to be positively self-determining when she became ill in 1923. Then she decided to 'take care' of her own health, to 'take advantage' of a famous doctor, and to 'fight' for a few more years. In 1932 she 'threw away' the doctors' medicines. Finally, there is the *contingency* model. A letter written in 1889 is full of thoughts about the course her life might have taken but for her obligations to her first husband: 'my occupations leave me no chance for the things I would naturally have chosen'. Later in 1918, she recognized that so long as she was 'prudent' then she could hope to avoid ill-health.

This analysis demonstrates how the experience of ageing is full of the changing images of life, past, present and future, and how this is reflected in the changing views of people as they age. Throughout her correspondence, Mary Berenson uses words and phrases in ways that are still familiar. Many of her own comments in her middle years are touched by ageism: ideas about decline and loss of control, and a sense of humiliation. It was only with illness that she became less fatalistic and self-deprecatory.

Assessing health needs

It is interesting now to contrast this kind of theorizing with that of textbooks. The following is a summarized amalgam of some current texts concerning the effective deployment of health services. A distinction is often made in health service planning between those conceptual frameworks that are tools to help in assessing health needs, and those frameworks that are theoretical, that encapsulate knowledge and understanding. It is the latter that represent an approach to theorizing that contrasts with that of the individual ageing person.

One concern of health service planners is with the age distribution of the population and, more generally, with demographic change. The life cycle has been as popular with planners as it was with nineteenth century evangelists. In introducing the life cycle framework, the following comment might be made:

This framework draws on well established biological concepts and incorporates a variety of theories about various social influences on health and health needs.

On this basis, a listing of life cycle groups might be compiled, each distinguished by chronological age and ending with:

Age group:	*Some key issues:*
75 years and over	multiple morbidity, dementia and depression, maintenance of function and independence, social isolation, quality of housing

This starkly represents the way in which, in endeavouring to meet the needs of the population as a whole, the planners of services are obliged to think and theorize in terms of mass age categories. On the basis of a framework that equates 75 years and over with multiple morbidity and social isolation, theories concerning the assessment of health needs are allowed to develop. In this way ageist stereotypes acquire a spurious scientific authority.

Basic models

How do we set about theorizing age? The first element in any theory about age is, of course, time. We see our lives mapped out on the continuous dimension of time. We measure the passage of time through the daily and annual cycles. By numbering and counting years we construct a basic measure of age. This presents us with two basic models of the life course shown in Figures 1 and 2.

Given these models, we can begin to theorize age by plotting other dimensions against it. A simple example is height against age (Figure 3). The facts are indisputable and we call the initial rise in height *growth*. So long as we think of growth simply as an increase in height and in other measures of physical size, then this theory is rudimentary and uncontentious. However, the word 'growth' is associated with other less tangible ideas. Essentially it has

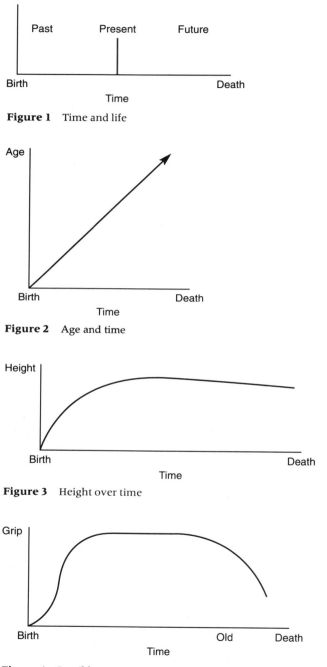

Figure 1   Time and life

Figure 2   Age and time

Figure 3   Height over time

Figure 4   Possible perception of grip over time

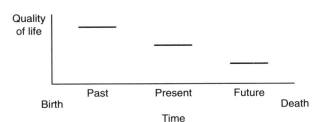

Figure 5   Possible perception of quality of life over time

Figure 6   Possible perception of quality of life by relative age

a certain ideological significance. Whether we are talking about the national economy or a child's vocabulary, growth is seen to be a positive thing.

If we now turn to negative things, an obvious example is the concept of *decline*. It is possible of course to collect empirical evidence that proves conclusively that there is a slight fall in average height in later life. But again, the word 'decline' means much more than a fall in some measurable quantity. When Mary Berenson visited her doctor, for example, he had in mind a model of decline which he applied to 'fat old ladies' and which is articulated as 'loosing their grip'. It would be depicted as in Figure 4. This is typical of the more general decline model. A high level of grip is valued and a low level is not. The decline in later life takes you from the desirable state of having grip to the undesirable one of having lost it. It is this kind of value judgement that is the basis of ageism.

The assumption is that the quality of life, as measured in all sorts of different ways, is reduced in later life. Although biologists would challenge this, the popular theory – well represented by Mary Berenson's experience – is that a general decline is the result of changes in body and mind. This kind of mapping is often referred to as a representation of the ageing process. The biological facts of life can, theoretically, be represented by a line on a graph. It is when a fall in this line, as in Figure 4, is interpreted as a decline rather than a change, that ageism compromises the scientist's objectivity.

The ageing individual can review life at a certain point in time. Rather than the elevated view of the whole life course that is implied in Figures 3 and 4, it is one oriented to the past-present-future conception of time as represented in Figure 5. Rather than a sense of process, this symbolizes a stark contrast between life in the past and the prospects of life in the future. Given this scenario, it is not surprising if we feel negative about the impact of ageing upon our lives.

Similarly we can translate the decline model of Figure 4 into a valuation of the lives of other people. By looking around, perhaps in the manner of Gladys Elder (page 38), we may view our acquaintances as in Figure 6. Again we can think sympathetically about older people and their sufferings, and we can see them as representing what is in prospect for ourselves.

Systematic research

Sociologists and other academic disciplines often make a distinction between macro and micro levels of analysis. In much of this book I have adopted a micro strategy starting at the level of the ageing individual, and yet much of the most powerful evidence regarding ageism is available at the macro level. Typically this begins with representative data covering the entire population. It is often argued that individuals are always idiosyncratic and that the generality of the experience of ageing can only be understood through the study of representative samples of the population at large.

Sometimes the resulting data is analysed with age as a continuous variable, producing graphs such as Figures 3 and 4, rather more precisely drawn but readily interpreted as representing the typical ageing process. More often, however, the population is broken down into age groups in order that something can be learnt about the impact of age upon different groups. So, in developing a framework for deploying health services, for example, information is obtained about the characteristics of age groups such as those aged 75 or over.

Poverty

A well-known example of systematic research at the macro level is Townsend's massive work on poverty (1979). In Chapter 16 of his book, Townsend focuses attention on thirteen social minorities, defined as:

- One-parent family
- Woman and adult dependant
- Large family
- Unemployed
- Households affected by the long-term sickness and injury of an adult under 65
- Households in which there is a disabled adult under 65
- Households in which there is a 'borderline' disabled adult under 65
- Households in which there is a disabled child
- Households in which there is a severely handicapped adult over 65
- Households with low-paid female earners
- Households with low-paid male earners
- Households in which there is a non-white person
- Households in which there is someone born in Eire

(Townsend 1979: 568–9)

Townsend selected some of these groups because they had been studied previously by other social scientists, others because they were the subject of popular discussion, and others because he had hypothesized that the incidence of poverty would be higher than average (p. 568). There follow seven chapters on poverty in the following groups:

- the unemployed and the sub-employed
- the low paid
- the older worker
- disabled people and the long-term sick
- handicapped children
- one-parent families
- old people.

These two typologies illustrate how sociologists working at the macro level, such as Townsend, use age as a means of defining groups that exist within the population. The focus of Townsend's attention is poverty, and theory contributes by explaining how age, *as a variable* distinguishing groups within the population, is associated with poverty.

His interest in historical trends is pitched only at the macro level of national policies, and he protests that too much attention has been given to the individual level of analysis:

> One tendency of research in recent years has been to limit explanation by studying the elderly as if they were independent of the economy and the polity and even of the general structure and value system of society . . . With some noteworthy exceptions, too little attention has been given both to comparisons between the elderly and the rest of the population and to the internal analysis of structural differences among the elderly.
>
> (Townsend 1979: 786)

He then produces the following table, defining 'elderly' as being of pensionable age. This demonstrates convincingly the substantially higher level of poverty among the elderly compared with the non-elderly:

Table 1   Income and age

Net disposable income as per cent of supplementary benefit standard plus housing cost	Elderly	Non-elderly
Under 100	20	7
100–139	44	19
140–199	17	31
200 or more	19	43
Number (= 100 per cent)	861	4,494

Source: Townsend 1979: 787

No other statistics are needed to prove the major social inequalities between age groups. This provides clear evidence that older people as a group suffer from extraordinarily high levels of poverty.

Poverty: older people who have no bank accounts, living in a village with no post office, being visited by a Poll Tax collecting van
Photograph: Mo Wilson

This approach to the study of age is based upon a theoretical framework that has age conceptualized as a structuring dimension within society, and the elderly as a definable group. Age is one of several such dimensions and, for each, research can reveal the extent of inequalities in income, employment, health and so on. In this way, the elderly can be placed alongside women, ethnic minorities and the disabled, as a social group that suffers deprivation and prejudice.

This theoretical approach is relevant to the study of ageism not just because of the proven deprivation but also because of the way in which the categories themselves are 'constructed' – and this means not just defined for operational purposes but also given ideological meaning. It is to this question that I turn in the next chapter.

9

No more 'elderly', no more old age

I indicated in Chapter 2 that the idea that old age or being elderly has some kind of universal reality needs to be challenged. Is it a condition, a period of life, a state of mind, or what? Is there any scientific evidence that something exists that can be called old age? If it exists, how do people enter it and become elderly?

It seems to me indisputable that a rethinking of ageism cannot be based upon the presumption that old age exists. And it follows directly from this, that we must critically examine the logic for creating a category of people and calling it the elderly, the old or the aged.

Unpacking Butler's definition

A rethinking of ageism also has to begin with Butler's definition (see page 30). The critical sentence is:

> Ageism can be seen as a process of systematic stereotyping of and discrimination against people because they are old, just as racism and sexism accomplish this for skin colour and gender.
>
> (Butler and Lewis 1973)

This was the kind of working definition that was needed in order to get ageism on the agenda in the 1960s. In the 1990s, however, it is inadequate and arguably ageist itself. Consider the key words.

Process

Process is used by Butler to represent an ongoing history of behaviours, practices, routines and regulations. While this undoubtedly is how ageism is made manifest, ageism itself is an ideology, not a process. Giddens defines ideology as:

> shared ideas or beliefs which serve to justify the interests of dominant groups. Ideologies are found in all societies in which there are systematic and engrained inequalities between groups.
>
> (Giddens 1989: 727)

It follows from this that an ideology is a coherent set of shared ideas and beliefs that constitute a particular justification of the interests of dominant groups. It is in this sense that ageism is an ideology upon which dominant groups − state, employers, hospitals, media, etc. − justify and sustain not just the inequalities between age groups but also the belief that these age groups exist and are different.

Systematic

The word 'systematic' in these definitions of ageism and ideology implies that stereotyping, discrimination and the generation of inequalities is undertaken according to some overall pattern, that the outcome of these processes is that the whole population is categorized according to rules and with some consistency. This confirms that the stereotyping and discrimination identified by Butler do constitute an ideology. Paradoxically, the word also suggests that this ideology is implemented indiscriminately to all those in the targeted groups. This aspect of ageist discrimination is often used to justify the use of age as a means of exclusion (see page 49 regarding the appointment of magistrates).

Stereotyping

Stereotyping is the attribution of a range of distinctive characteristics to all members of a group. Butler suggests that old people are 'categorized as senile, rigid in thought and manner, and old fashioned in morality and skills'. There are two important aspects to stereotyping which need to be distinguished. One is the ascription of negative characteristics. Terms such as imbecility, senile, rigid and old fashioned, are viewed negatively in popular opinion; most of us would feel offended if they were applied to ourselves. The second aspect is that stereotyping draws upon generalization, and possibly upon valid scientific research. For example, 'old people are typically poor' is the kind of conclusion that might be drawn from Townsend's data (see page 113), and indeed might form the basis of anti-ageist action. Nevertheless, this concluding statement, and the word 'typically' in particular, can foster the belief that 'all old people are poor': a classic stereotype which fosters a wide range of ageist responses such as concessionary travel fares and Christmas bonuses.

Discrimination

Discrimination is action taken in relation to all members of a certain group. The Invalid Care Allowance is an obvious example of ageist discrimination (page

5): the carers of recipients must be under 65 to receive the Allowance. Typically, discrimination is viewed negatively, but there is always a positive interpretation. For example, it might be claimed that the ICA is being targeted upon those whose carers might otherwise be unavailable due to paid employment. Concessionary fares for older people are a form of positive discrimination that, from time to time, many younger people resent. The important point about discrimination is that it occurs through the power to systematically exclude individuals belonging to designated categories.

They

Who are 'we' and who are 'they'? Kuhn, in a discussion of being old in an ageist culture, asserts 'we are a new breed of old people' (1977: 14). In contrast, 'we', for other writers, are service providers:

> Our society has a very negative attitude towards old age. This affects the way we treat elderly people, the expectations we have of them and the services we provide.
>
> (Dixon and Gregory 1987: 20)

The use of these pronouns creates a conceptual map on which groups of people are variously included and excluded. In particular, the old who are discriminated against occupy a different territory on these us/them maps from 'us'. This issue is amplified below.

Old

The main reference to age in Butler's definition is through the word 'old'. His conceptualization of ageism is related to a discernible group of people who can be referred to as old. He, like many others, uses a number of other words to refer to this group – older, elders, elderly, aged – but not in a way which challenges the presumption of its existence. Again this is discussed in more detail below.

Sexism and racism

Butler's reference to sexism and racism is near universal practice in writing about ageism. The two words 'just as' directly imply equivalence, thereby ignoring what is distinctive and peculiar about age. As Cole has commented about ageism, 'We do not yet have the careful, critical scholarship that might justify or illuminate its analogies to racism or sexism' (Cole 1986: 119).

Others, fearing that age discrimination might be perceived to be no more than the latest fashion, are cautious about adding ageism to the anti-discriminatory agenda (Stevenson 1989: 8). Despite the obvious advantage that can be gained through exploiting the equivalence with sexism and racism, well demonstrated by Laslett (1989) in commenting on Medawar and Gould (page 26), the equivalence itself is no basis for a definition. As soon as that is agreed, then we have to address the question of what it is about age in society, rather than the position of older people, that is unacceptable.

What this brief analysis implies is that Butler's definition is inadequate on three grounds: i) a definition of ageism should not be based on parallels with sexism and racism; ii) it should not presume that old people exist as a group; iii) it fails to resolve the us/them question.

Us and them

The distinction between us and them, of course, reflects the contrast between the subjective and the objective. In talking about people born in Yorkshire, for example, I have a choice of talking about 'we' and our attachment to certain cultural eccentricities or I can talk about 'them' and their attachment, etc. Even though the latter does not necessarily exclude me as being one of them, the objective grammar allows a certain distancing. The word 'them' establishes a distinction between the implied 'we' and them. So, when Butler refers to 'discrimination against people because they are old', he is creating the same distinction: between a kind of ageless 'we' (ageless in the sense that our age is considered irrelevant) and 'them' who are old. The alternative was:

Ageism can be seen as a process of systematic stereotyping of and discrimination against us when we are considered old . . .

The problem with this, of course, is that it implies a concern with ourselves and our future selves, rather than with older people currently suffering the consequences of ageism.

Service providers, in particular, are aware that there are categories of people who are in urgent need and, in the documentation of policy and practice, it is perhaps inevitable that there is constant reference to 'them and their needs' and to 'us and our services'. The copywriter of the advertisement at the beginning of Chapter 7 (page 88) attempted to overcome this with the popular 'one day you'll be old too' theme. However, this simply emphasized the size of the typical age difference between provider and recipient.

Categorization

Is there any clinical evidence of a biological change that marks the onset of an old age characterized by an indisputable degree of need? Grimley Evans (1991) would appear to suggest not.

Ageing of an organism is characterised by loss of adaptability; as time passes its homeostatic mechanisms become less sensitive, slower, less accurate, and less well sustained. The onset and rate of these changes vary among bodily systems and, because aging is the result of interaction between extrinsic (environmental) and intrinsic (genetic) factors, there is also great variation between individuals. Death is the ultimate failure of adaptability, and senescence first becomes detectable in population data as a rise in age specific mortality at the age of 12 to 13. After perturbations due to violent deaths in early adult life mortality increases roughly exponentially for the rest of life.

There is no discontinuity to offer a biological basis for separating 'the elderly' from the rest of the adult human race. The prevalence of disability and the use of health and social services also increase broadly exponentially through adult life, with no discontinuity in later life.

(Grimley Evans 1991: 869)

In effect he subscribes to the view that there is a wide range of conditions for which the attention of a medically qualified doctor is appropriate and which are strongly associated in the statistical sense with age, but that in no circumstance should a person's age compromise the medical response.

People often express confidence in the existence of old age, not on physiological but on cultural grounds. Every society has had a concept of old age. We can't simply decide that it doesn't exist any more. Who are we to dispute the Greeks, the Romans and the Bible?

The problem is that what we know about the understanding of age in ancient societies is what has survived hundreds of acts of editorial selection, control and translation. Often, to give sense to what has been written, the term 'old age' has had to be used. And even supposing that we share the same understanding of what old age is, how often did these ancient writers themselves use the concept of old age uncritically, *following* rather than leading the usage of the general populace?

Stages

Arguably old age has only existed as a result of the urge to divide the life course up into stages. Minois refers to the stage theories of the Middle Ages as 'abstract dissertations, intellectuals' games, which did not correspond with any practical distinctions' (1989: 5) and Cole argues that in the past old age was not a stage of life that was set apart by ritual or customs (1992: 11). Likewise Achenbaum has noted that historians have begun to investigate:

the possibility that each stage of life has a history that is unique, or at least one that develops somewhat independently of continuities and permutations in the evolution of other stages.

(Achenbaum 1978: 1)

In other words, old age is a cultural concept, a construction that has a certain popular utility in sustaining ageism within societies that need scapegoats. Likewise Bromley could have challenged the idea of old age in much the same way as he undermined the validity of the concept of middle age:

The term 'middle age' does not refer to any well-defined stage in the human life-cycle and it means different things to different people . . . Nevertheless, middle age is a convenient fiction in so far as it points to an important aspect of adult psychology . . .

(Bromley 1988: 158)

Replace middle age with old age and the argument is clear: to be well-defined, old age would need to have a clearly identifiable beginning and ending – like life itself, for example. Clearly it doesn't have and so we are all free to make what we will of it. But why are these ideas 'a convenient fiction'? Is it because they serve to reinforce ageism?

Old people as a group

To argue against the elderly being identified as a social group could be seen as undermining their political strength. What hope is there if elderly people are not encouraged to take collective political action themselves? How can those committed to a well-resourced and fair welfare state ensure that wealth is redistributed to the poorest groups in society if it is to be claimed that the largest such group does not actually exist?

There are two answers to this. The first is that people should be free to associate and take collective action in whatever name they choose. If the pensioner's movement in the UK chooses to call itself The National Association of the Elderly, so be it. It is significant of course that it does not. What about 'senior citizens'? Some like to be called that when they join a local club. Again, no one could object if that is how the members of the club want to be known. But there is a question over how they came to acquire that name: it could be chosen by a town council wanting to be seen to be looking after its senior citizens.

What about pensioners? Is it not right that the pensioners' movement should take collective action as pensioners? This is different from the elderly and senior citizens: pensioners receive a pension and for most this is their main source of income. In the UK, the state pension is outrageously low in comparison with the average wage nationally and with state pensions in other countries. All state pensioners should unite and take collective action. This, supported by sympathizers of course, is potentially the most effective strategy for ensuring that the pension becomes the basis of an adequate income. There is here a clear and unambiguous grievance that directly affects some individuals and not others.

This prompts the second answer. Evidence of ageism is clearly apparent in statistics such as those compiled by Townsend (page 113). Information about poverty among older people is essential in the fight against ageism. But, rather than 'elderly' and 'non-elderly', the columns in Townsend's tables should have labels that relate directly to the categories being tabulated: people over pensionable age and people under. Only then do we know precisely what sectors of the population are being analysed.

To summarize, in rethinking ageism we have to recognize that we are all ageing, are all of an age, and are all vulnerable to ageism. In addition, however, we must understand that ageism affects different groups differently. First, there are those in particular circumstances – residents in old people's homes or pensioners, for example – and they have particular battles with ageism to fight. It is right that those who are not in such homes and not in receipt of a pension should provide them with support but not to presume to share the same experience: 'I understand' can be an oppressive and presumptuous expression of solidarity. Second, evidence of mass ageism is available in the statistics that contrast different age groups. We should not be ignorant of the fact that 64 per cent of people of pensionable age in the UK (over six million people) receive a

Pensioners' action: a Maxwell victim listens attentively at the first full-scale meeting between a government minister and the dead tycoon's swindled pensioners
Photograph: Don McPhee © *The Guardian*

net disposable income that is less than the widely accepted poverty level, and of the implications of this for the quality of their lives. It is in these two ways that the us/them divide is not ageist.

The institutional context

It is important to recognize that the ageism of individuals does not necessarily arise out of an innate prejudice or dislike of the old. It is not some characteristic that we are born with – a fear of ageing – which makes us shy away from any involvement with older people. Individual ageism arises from two sources: the culture into which we are socialized and the contexts in which we are sometimes obliged to engage with older people. Much of this book has focused upon the first of these. In this section I want to discuss the second.

I think of context here as a socio-spatial phenomenon: how people interact within a limited space. Consider a tangible example. Much of our lives is spent in rooms. A room is a physically enclosed space: four walls, a floor and a ceiling. Contact with the outside world is achieved through window, door, telephone and sometimes through the wall. Most rooms are used for particular purposes and they are furnished accordingly. Sometimes they are used for other purposes and then conflict may arise. Sometimes there is someone in charge who ensures that behaviour is in accordance with the intended use, someone who also regulates entries and exits. Within the one room, there is a continuing history of movements in and out and of social contacts between people.

The first point I would make is that the room – and probably the whole building in which it is located – is normally owned by one individual or organization, and the owner plays a large part in determining who has access, and what use is made of the room. Part of the reason for the construction of the room is to provide a barrier between those inside and those outside. People normally enter the room through the door, and the owner may make the room secure with a lock on the door, at the same time as deciding who should possess a key. In determining the use that is made of the room, the owner will decorate it and furnish it appropriately with furniture and equipment.

Now let us suppose that the owner decides on a particular use which gives controlled access to two classes of individuals: clients and agents. The owner appoints the agents, sometimes employs and pays them, and requires them to perform various functions serving the interests of either owner and/or clients. This specification would cover an enormous range of different kinds of rooms: lodging rooms, prison cells, hospital wards, church halls, ballrooms, corner shops, executive offices, lifts, school classrooms, telephone boxes – the list is endless. Sometimes the agent engages in social interaction with clients. Sometimes, the agent is simply required to hold the key and control access. Sometimes visitors are admitted to the room – people who are neither clients nor agents.

Age restrictions

What are the consequences if agents are instructed to exclude all prospective clients outside a specified age range? I would suggest that whatever the situation, whatever the reason, this characteristic represents institutional ageism, imposed upon both the agents and the clients. The agent, for example, is required to exclude one person who is just 12 months too young and to admit another who is only two years older – regardless of their respective needs of, or contribution to, the activities being undertaken in the room.

It is important to appreciate that the consequence of such ageism is far more serious than just that of determining the criteria for admission. The control procedure itself has a profound impact upon the perceptions of all concerned of

A room for 'the elderly'
Photograph: Melanie Friend, Format

the character and the reasons for the activities that go on in the room. Indeed, the procedure may be undertaken at the door itself and, as a result, the act of exclusion may be witnessed by all those inside. The activities and the room become identified with the age bar as well as with the clients themselves and so, of course, do the agents. As soon as we label the clients 'the elderly', then the vocabulary of the world of the room becomes decided: we have activities for the elderly in the room for the elderly, being undertaken by the elderly, using aids for the elderly with the support of workers or carers of the elderly. For clients, agents, visitors, those refused entry, and for all those others with whom these people share their other social worlds, what goes on in the room comes to symbolize the meaning of 'elderly': a stereotyping image develops of the life and character of the elderly. The ageism that draws upon this stereotype, reinforced by personal observation and testimony of what goes on in the room, engulfs the subsequent lives of not just the clients, the elderly themselves, but of all those acquainted with the world of the room. The room makes the label tangible: 'Dad? Oh, he's down with the elderly!'

'Is there an alternative?'

'Yes: a room intended for older people.'

'Isn't that just a euphemism for elderly people?'

'No, it's for older people not elderly people.'

'I don't understand – what do you mean older people?'

'Just that – older people.'

'But how do you define older.'

'Older is older.'

'Now you're being stupid: would you admit a 20-year-old?'

'Yes.'

'A five-year-old?'

'Yes.'

'Right, so what's to stop it being taken over by a whole gang of aggressive teenagers?'

'Nothing except the fact that the owner says the room is for older people.'

'So what do you do if that happens?'

'Well, if there's an alternative room that is designated for younger people, I might suggest that they go there instead. If there is still an excessive demand for entry, an assessment procedure can be devised that takes account of age without designating people as elderly and without barring those who are not old enough. We may find that the youngest client, having gained entry primarily through other criteria, is 40 years of age, say. Nevertheless the average age of the clients may still be 70-something. They are indisputably older people, even though no one, not even a 5-year-old is automatically barred.'

'So that's how you would organize any kind of service for older people?'

'Yes.'

Taking on ageism

In our article on defining ageism (Bytheway and Johnson 1990), we put forward four suggestions for anti-ageist action. First, we should abandon ageist language. In particular, we should abandon the word 'elderly' and begin to use a relative rather than an absolute age vocabulary. In March 1993, I spent an hour expounding the argument against 'elderly' and 'old age' to a group of 21 students from eleven different countries who were attending a short course in social gerontology at the International Institute of Ageing in Malta. They quickly agreed that there was no point at which someone became elderly and that this invalidated categorizations of people as elderly. They were reluctant, however, to let go of the word itself. They recognized that the alternative *older* was relative, was not exclusionary, did not set people apart, but they wanted to retain 'elderly'. 'People get grey hair, they are more frail, they need services, we need a name for it', one said.

'What is this *it*?', I countered. 'I don't deny we all grow older. I don't deny that people in their nineties are of a great age and that most have real needs. I don't deny we need a technical vocabulary, but what is this *it* that has to be called "elderly"?'

Second, we should recognize age for what it is. Upon reading this, a colleague astutely asked us what age is. In truth our suggestion was a limply worded acknowledgement that certain things are undeniable. No matter how committed one is to the social constructionist approach, there comes a point when one has to face the reality in front of one's eyes and, indeed, the reality of the condition of one's much-used body. The following section addresses this issue.

Third, we should stop using age as an institutional regulator. As I have suggested at various points in this book, age bars are ageist. Fourth, we should abandon the us–them mentality. We should begin to think in inclusionary ways, seeing ourselves in a broader temporal context, in terms of our lives as a whole rather than our lives at present.

Realism

What then is the reality of age? What about the physical condition of older people and, in particular, very old people? You cannot deny that many are frail and that they have declined both physically and mentally. As Grimley Evans observed (pages 118–19), there are all sorts of changes that come. Regardless of individual and group variation, there are many measurable characteristics that change according to a set, almost universal, pattern. The critical point is that the body of an 80-year-old is unmistakably not that of a 20-year-old and vice versa: the visible evidence, even when a person is fully clothed, is indisputable. Certainly I would not dispute it. But it's a lifetime of change, not a momentary change, that generates the difference: this is the fact. Where ageism comes in is, in our pathetic attempts to be certain about the changes that come with age, in the assumption that they are all universal, in our efforts to distance ourselves from those who appear different, in our negative interpretations and in the consequential regulation of the social order.

If we are to be effective in challenging ageism, we have to recognize the significance of *difference*. Perhaps the following account (Macdonald and Rich 1983: 7–12) of the personal discovery of ageism will demonstrate the import-ance of this. It also reveals the potential we all have for being thoroughly ageist in our relations with older people and, in particular, in our ability to conceptualize them as being apart from us.

Through their involvement in the women's movement in the USA, Cynthia Rich had got to know Barbara Macdonald – 21 years her senior – in 1974. Regarding her knowledge of ageism at that time, Rich writes:

> 'Ageism' is hardly a word in my vocabulary. It has something to do with job discrimination in middle age. And aging itself I see as simply 'failing', a painful series of losses, an inevitable confrontation with the human condition.
>
> (Macdonald and Rich 1983: 10)

Feeling part of the women's movement – 'we are all women together' – and having noticed that other older friends had never talked about ageing, she had assumed that they had 'transcended' it. 'I could have the illusion of the richness of difference without having to confront the reality of difference' (Macdonald and Rich 1983: 9). After living with Rich for three years, Macdonald began to write about ageism in 1977, and it was only then that Rich became aware of her own ageism:

> Slowly, I begin to see that the fear of the stigma of age, and total ignorance of its reality in the lives of old women, flow deep in myself, in other women I know, in the women's movement. That our society breeds ignorance and fear of both aging and death. That the old woman carries the burden of that stigma, and with remarkable, unrecognized, unrecorded courage. I begin to see that I myself am aging, was always aging, and that only powerful forces could have kept me – from self-interest alone – from working to change the social and economic realities of older women. That ageism is part of the air both Barbara and I have breathed since we were born, and that it is unthinkable that women should continue to be indifferent to the meaning of the whole of our lives, until we are old ourselves.
>
> (Macdonald and Rich 1983: 11–12)

This powerful statement sustains the distinctiveness of old women – as remarkable, unrecognized, unrecorded, courageous people. It could be argued that the use of 'old' not 'older' emphasizes not just difference but also a distinction between us and them. Be that as it may, it also asserts loudly that ageing is a shared experience, that we are all subject to the fear and ignorance of ageism, and that the power of ageism should be challenged in ways that promote a holistic and undivided view of 'the whole of our lives'.

It seemed to me in studying their book, that this was their central message and that any attack on ageism had to tackle the ideological and cultural division between us and them – however defined. It meant that, in the writing of this book, I have endeavoured to ensure that I did not foster the continued conceptualization of older people as 'them'. I have learnt to think in terms of younger and older people in ways which do not require reference to us and them; to consider the relations between generations which are historically defined; and to accept that where eligibility for particular services is defined on age grounds (i.e. is intrinsically ageist), it does not follow that service providers who refer to their clients as them are ageist too and, indeed, that it can be presumptuous to claim to understand the situation and experience of the eligible.

Expectation of life

Consider one other simple but fundamental contrast that might be made between the elderly and the non-elderly: their expectation of life. The statistical facts are well-known: an infant, born in Britain in 1993, can expect nearly 80 years of future life, but the 65-year-old can expect less than 20 years. What a contrast! One individual with the whole of life ahead; the other with the greater part of it gone. This is not ageist prejudice. The facts are indisputable. How can facts be ageist?

Well, the answer lies in the question: why measure life expectation only at 0 years and 65 years? Why not compare the life expectations of the 13-year-old and the 23-year-old; or the 78-year-old and the 88-year-old? What is so special about the ages 0 and 65? The justification might go as follows:

> *Life expectation at age 0 is the expected length of a whole life. This is what we can expect: nearly 80 years of life. At age 65, however, we become members of the elderly population: our working lives are over. This is a whole new world and we can expect less than 20 years in which to make the best of it.*

The life expectation statistic summarizes the overall levels of age-specific mortality in a population at one particular point in time. Yet it is designed to be interpreted personally as in the above reasoning. By comparing age 0 years with age 65 years, we are fostering the ageist idea that old age is life in a different country, it's the life of a different species. The would-be hard-headed realist will argue that no amount of thinking positive ('When you're 65 you still have 20, 30 or even more years ahead of you!') can alter the inference that elderly people are different from us. However, as soon as we abandon the ideas that old age exists and that the age of 65 is in some way special, then it becomes possible to represent changing expectations of life rather more sensitively, demonstrating how it constantly changes as one moves along the age scale and how there is no marked change at any particular age to substantiate the archaic category of elderly people.

A certain fascination has developed regarding the 'rectangularization' of mortality (Fries and Crapo 1981). What this represents is simply a recognition that death is increasingly occurring within a narrow age range in later life. Regardless of the debates of the biologists, it is clear that we can all increasingly expect a full life of about 80 years. There is a certain justice in the ideal of everyone attaining the same fixed length of life. It could hardly be ageist if, in accordance with Osler's recommendation, we died naturally and automatically upon reaching our sixty-first birthday although, in this day and age, we may prefer Fries' limit of 85 years.

The fact is, however, that reality is more complicated, even when – and arguably *particularly* when – variation is reducing. It is reasonable to assert that everyone, no matter how old, ill or weak they may be, can hope for at least one more day of life. It may be that doctors, taking account of a certain set of symptoms, history and other clinical evidence, would aim more for amelioration than cure for an older person than for a younger person. If this practice is based upon clinical judgement, taking full account of the possible benefits and risks of the alternatives, then it reflects more a recognition of the physical realities of age rather than the power of ageism. When, however, treatments are systematically barred to people over a certain age because of a presumption that there will be no benefit, or because younger people are automatically given priority, or because limited success could lead to a continuing burden, then this is institutionalized ageism.

Being positive

So, in defiance of ageism, should we think positive? Within the old age industry, there are many who urge us to do so. They come from many different quarters: from health education to the travel industry. Many textbooks in gerontology promote a positive view of human ageing. There is a certain salvationist zeal in much of this literature. USE IT OR LOSE IT! – there are many slogans.

Often writers report that when acquaintances learn that they work with older people, the comment is: it must be depressing. 'We must challenge these attitudes!', they proclaim. 'We must challenge the negative stereotypes of old age!' They then offer many examples of hearty or heroic elders to add inspiration to the pages that follow.

In the language of this rhetoric, positive means good means happiness means liking, and negative means bad means misery means disliking. The people who act positive are those we like. Expressed in this way, the emphasis on positive attitudes can be particularly invidious when we exercise the powers we have to benefit only those we like.

It is also not difficult to see in this anti-ageist positivism an element of knowing what's best for them, believing we know all the answers, blaming others for their ignorance and misery, and seeking to save them through exhortation and example. Given this, Cole is quite right when he argues that ageism and its critics represent the alternating voices of a fugue on the theme of growing old (Cole 1992: 228).

So I would argue that it is a fundamental mistake to equate an anti-ageist stance with thinking positive. But this is not to say that we should resist being positive. The sceptic always runs the risk of being branded negative, but there are ways of being positive which do not promote idealized scenarios and unreal beliefs. Rather than claim that:

> *Most elderly people are really nice, absolutely fascinating once you get to know them . . . The things they say! . . . Working with them is really interesting . . . Some of them are real characters!*

It is far less patronizing, far less self-righteous and far less ageist, to state that:

> *The people I work with are pretty ordinary. They have lived long lives and survived many experiences. I like working with them because there are things I can do to make life more satisfactory for them. They tell me what they think and I listen to them and sometimes argue. You can learn a lot from ordinary people. I enjoy the work; it's worth doing.*

Recommended reading

If ageism is to be taken seriously, it is important that a good and critical literature develops. Implicit in this, of course, is the need for that literature to be read and studied. This is a long but highly selective list of recommended reading with some brief annotated comments.

Arber, S. and Ginn, J. (1991) *Gender and Later Life*. London: Sage.
  Chapters 2 and 3 provide an up-to-date review of ageism in the late 1980s, with particular reference to gender.
Beauvoir, S. de (1977) *Old Age*. Harmondsworth: Penguin.
  An essential work in the study of ageism, providing an historical and global perspective.
Biggs, S. (1989) *Confronting Ageing*. London: Central Council for Education and Training in Social Work.
  A useful training aid for tackling attitudes to age.
Bond, J., Coleman, P. and Peace S. (eds) (1993) *Ageing in Society*. London: Sage publications.
  Valuable up-to-date social gerontology textbook.
Bornat, J., Phillipson, C. and Ward, S. (1985) *A Manifesto for Old Age*. London: Pluto Press.
  A book needing to be re-issued; a review of pressures upon pensioners in the UK in the early 1980s followed by a manifesto directed at 'a future Labour government'.
Bromley, D. B. (ed.) (1984) *Gerontology: Social and Behavioural Perspectives*. London: Croom Helm.
  Includes Itzin's chapter on 'The double jeopardy of ageism and sexism: media images of women'.
Butler, R. N. (1975) *Why Survive? Being Old in America*. New York: Harper and Row.
  A comprehensive and detailed account of prejudice and discrimination against old people in the United States in the early 1970s.
Bytheway, B. (1990) The concept of age, in Peace, S. M. (ed.) *Researching Social Gerontology: Concepts, Methods and Issues*. London: Sage, for British Society of Gerontology, 9–18.

In this paper, I discuss the concept of old age beginning with its measurement. I suggest links between the social construction of stages such as old age and the development of gerontology.

Bytheway, B. and Johnson, J. (1990) On defining ageism, *Critical Social Policy*, 27, 27–39.
A discussion of the nature of ageism – this book develops this earlier discussion.

Callahan, D. (1987) *Setting Limits: Medical Goals in an Aging Society*. New York: Simon and Schuster.
A basic text in the debate on age rationing.

Carver, V. and Liddiard, P. (1978) *An Ageing Population*. Milton Keynes: Open University Press.
Still a challenging reader, including Sontag on 'The double standard of ageing'; Hendricks and Hendricks on 'Ageism and common stereotypes'; Slater on 'Age discrimination'.

Cole, T. R. (1992) *The Journey of Life: A Cultural History of Aging in America*. Cambridge: Cambridge University Press.
The epilogue to this book contains an important critique of the anti-ageist movement.

Coupland, N., Coupland, J. and Giles, H. (1991) *Language, Society and the Elderly*. Oxford: Basil Blackwell.
An important technical study of language and ageism.

Daniels, N. (1988) *Am I My Parents' Keeper?* Oxford: Oxford University Press.
An essay on justice between the young and the old.

Elder, G. (1977) *The Alienated: Growing Old Today*. London: Writers and Readers Publishing Cooperative.
A courageous review of being old in the UK in the 1970s.

Estes, C. (1979) *The Aging Enterprise*. San Francisco, CA: Jossey-Bass.
'In using the term *aging enterprise*, I hope to call particular attention to how the aged are often processed and treated as a commodity in our society and to the fact that the age-segregated policies that fuel the aging enterprise are socially divisive "solutions" that single out, stigmatize, and isolate the aged from the rest of society' (p. 2).

Fennell, G., Phillipson, C. and Evers, H. (1988) *The Sociology of Old Age*. Milton Keynes: Open University Press.
A useful raising of issues, including a discussion of how sociology has neglected the study of age.

Ford, J. and Sinclair, R. (1987) *Sixty Years On: Women Talk about Old Age*. London: The Women's Press.
A valuable ethnographic study of the lives of older women.

Forster, M. (1989) *Have the Men Had Enough?* London: Chatto and Windus.
One of the most important contemporary novels in portraying the experience of dementia.

Friedan, B. (1993) *The Fountain of Age*. London: Jonathan Cape.
A tremendous travelogue through current gerontological issues.

The Gerontologist. The journal of the (American) Gerontological Society. The location of many important papers in the development of the study of ageism (see Chapter 3 of this book).

Godlove, C., Richard, L. and Rodwell, G. (1982) *Time for Action*. Social Services Monographs: Research in Practice, University of Sheffield.
An observational study of day centres and residential homes, confirming the huge potential of empirical research in exposing ageism.

Greer, G. (1991) *The Change: Women, Ageing and the Menopause*. London: Hamish Hamilton.
A challenging review of knowledge and practices associated with the menopause, set in the context of a positive approach to the second half of life.

The Hen Co-op (1993) *Growing Old Disgracefully*. London: Judy Piatkus Publishers.

New ideas for getting the most out of life presented by six women who attended a special course for older people at a women's study centre in Lincolnshire.

Johnson, J. and Slater, R. (eds) (1993) *Ageing and Later Life*. London: Sage publications. Reader for *An Ageing Society* (Open University K256). Fifty-five chapters include personal accounts of ageing as well as discussions and analyses of ageism in modern Britain.

Johnson, P., Conrad, C. and Thomson, D. (1989) *Workers versus Pensioners*. Manchester: Manchester University Press.
An important book regarding intergenerational relations.

Laczko, F. and Phillipson, C. (1991) *Changing Work and Retirement*. Buckingham: Open University Press.
An up-to-date review of trends in the employment and retirement of older workers. It discusses the institutionalization of early exit from the labour force.

Laslett, P. (1989) *A Fresh Map of Life: The Emergence of the Third Age*. London: Weidenfeld and Nicolson.
The case for recognizing the Third Age: a remarkable and challenging analysis of historical trends.

Levin, J. and Levin, W. C. (1980) *Ageism: Prejudice and Discrimination against the Elderly*. Belmont, CA: Wadsworth.
An important book by two sociologists reviewing the development of gerontology and arguing that the discipline has tended to explain 'the problems of the aged as consequences of the individual's deterioration and decline' (p. ix).

Macdonald, B. and Rich, C. (1983) *Look Me in the Eye: Old Women, Aging and Ageism*. London: The Women's Press.
The essential book on ageism. An account of discovering and experiencing it, provided by two women of different ages.

McEwen, E. (1990) *Age: The Unrecognised Discrimination*. London: Age Concern.
A series of papers issued by Age Concern including a chapter by Scrutton on ageism.

Meade, C. (1987) *The Thoughts of Betty Spital: Pensioner Activist and Radical Granny*. Castleford: Yorkshire Arts Circus.
A book that is more disturbing than witty, it makes a powerful case for taking ageism seriously.

Minois, G. (1989) *History of Old Age*. Cambridge: Polity Press.
Perhaps the most comprehensive book on the history of age prejudice.

Peace, S. M. (ed.) (1990) *Researching Social Gerontology: Concepts, Methods and Issues*. London: Sage, for British Society of Gerontology.
Includes my paper on 'Age' in which I argue that ageism has developed through the social construction of age stages.

Phillipson, C. (1982) *Capitalism and the Construction of Old Age*. Basingstoke: Macmillan.
An important and early contribution to the political economy approach to the study of old age.

Phillipson, C. and Walker, A. (1986) *Ageing and Social Policy*. Aldershot: Gower Press.
A significant collection of papers bringing together social policy and gerontology.

Phillipson, C., Bernard, M. and Strang, P. (eds) (1986) *Dependency and Interdependency in Old Age: Theoretical Perspectives and Policy Alternatives*. London: Croom Helm.
A collection of BSG conference papers including Itzin's 'Ageism awareness training: a model for group work'.

Sarton, M. (1983) *As We Are Now*. London: The Women's Press.
A tremendous novel: residential care seen through the eyes of a resident.

Shapiro, J. (1989) *Ourselves, Growing Older: Women Ageing with Knowledge and Power*. London: Fontana.
A British edition of the volume produced by the Boston Women's Health Collective, authors of *Our Bodies Ourselves*.

Spicker, S. F., Woodward, K. M. and van Tassel, D. D. (1978) *Aging and the Elderly: Humanist Perspectives in Gerontology*. Atlantic Highlands, NJ: Humanities Press.

Another good reader including Gerald Gruman on 'Cultural origins of present-day ageism'.

Townsend, P. (1981) The structured dependency of the elderly: creation of social policy in the twentieth century', *Ageing and Society*, 1(1) 5–28.

The theory of structured dependency introduced: the connection to ageism is obvious if unstated.

Walker, A. (1990) The economic burden of ageing and the prospect of intergenerational conflict, *Ageing and Society*, 10(4) 377–96.

An important review of the debate over intergenerational conflict.

Warnes, A. M. (1993) Being old, old people and the burden of burdens, *Ageing and Society*, 13(3) 297–338.

A comprehensive analysis of the history, meanings and use of the word *burden*: a word that is central to ageism.

References

Achenbaum, W. A. (1978) *Old Age in the New Land*. Baltimore, MD: The Johns Hopkins University Press.

Arber, S. and Gilbert, N. (1989) Men: The forgotten carers. *Sociology*, 23(1) 111–18.

Arber, S. and Ginn, J. (1990) The meaning of informal care: gender and the contribution of elderly people. *Ageing and Society*, 10(4) 429–54.

Arber, S. and Ginn, J. (1991) *Gender and Later Life*. London: Sage.

Banks, T. (1992) Foreword. *Carnegie Inquiry into the Third Age*. London: Centre for Policy on Ageing.

Barron, M. L. (1953) Minority group characteristics of the aged in American society, *Journal of Gerontology*, 8, 477–82.

Barry, R. L. and Bradley, G. V. (1991) *Set No Limits: A rebuttal of Daniel Callahan's proposal to limit health care for the elderly*. Urbana, IL: University of Illinois Press.

Beauvoir, S. de (1977) *Old Age*. Harmondsworth: Penguin.

Benefits Agency (1993) *Benefits After Retirement*. Heywood, CA: BA Publications.

Biggs, S. (1989) *Confronting Ageing*. London: Central Council for Education and Training in Social Work.

Blaikie, A. (1990) The emerging political power of the elderly in Britain 1908–1948. *Ageing and Society*, 10(1) 17–40.

Blakemore, K. and Boneham, M. (1993) *Age, Race and Ethnicity*. Buckingham: Open University Press.

Bond, J., Coleman, P. and Peace, S. (eds) (1993) *Ageing in Society*. London: Sage publications.

Bornat, J., Phillipson, C. and Ward, S. (1985) *A Manifesto for Old Age*. London: Pluto Press.

Brecher, E. M. (1993) Love, sex and aging, in Johnson, J. and Slater, R. (eds) *Ageing and Later Life*. London: Sage publications, 107–11.

Brett, S. (1987) *The Faber Book of Diaries*. London: Faber and Faber.

Bromley, D. B. (ed.) (1984) *Gerontology: Social and Behavioural Perspectives*. London: Croom Helm.

Bromley, D. B. (1988) *The Psychology of Human Ageing*. Third Edition. Harmondsworth: Penguin.

Bury, M. (1988) Arguments about ageing: Long life and its consequences, in Wells, N. E. J. and Freer, C.B. (eds) *The Ageing Population: Burden or Challenge?* Basingstoke: Macmillan, 17–32.

Butler, R. N. (1975) *Why Survive? Being Old in America.* New York: Harper and Row.

Butler, R. N. (1978) Humanistic perspectives in gerontology, in Spicker, S. F., Woodward, K. M. and van Tassel, D. D. (eds) *Aging and the Elderly: Humanist Perspectives in Gerontology.* Atlantic Highlands, NJ: Humanities Press, 389–92.

Butler, R. N. (1980) Ageism: a foreword. *Journal of Social Issues*, 36(2) 8–11.

Butler. R. N. and Lewis, M. I. (1973) *Aging and Mental Health.* St Louis, MD: C. V. Mosby.

Bytheway, B. (1980) Is ageism just a joke? *New Age*, 12, 29–30.

Bytheway, B. (1981) Variation with age of age differences in marriage. *Journal of Marriage and the Family.* 43, 923–7.

Bytheway, B. (1982) Review symposium, *Ageing and Society*, 2(3) 389–91.

Bytheway, B. (1986) Making way: the disengagement of older workers, in Phillipson, C., Bernard, M. and Strang, P. (eds) *Dependency and Interdependency in Old Age: Theoretical Perspectives and Policy Alternatives.* London: Croom Helm, 315–26.

Bytheway, B. (1987) Redundancy and the older worker, in Lee, R. M. (ed.) *Redundancies, Lay-off and Plant Closures: Causes, Character and Consequences.* London: Croom Helm, 84–115.

Bytheway, B. (1990) The concept of age, in Peace, S. M. (ed.) *Researching Social Gerontology: Concepts, Methods and Issues.* London: Sage, for British Society of Gerontology, 9–18.

Bytheway, B. (1993a) Ageing and biography: the letters of Bernard and Mary Berenson, *Sociology*, 27, 153–65.

Bytheway, B. (1993b) Post-conference reflections. *Generations Review*, 3(4) 20–1.

Bytheway, B. (1993c) *Old Age and Ageism.* Unit 2, An Ageing Society (K256). Milton Keynes: The Open University.

Bytheway, B. and Johnson, J. (1990) On defining ageism, *Critical Social Policy*, 27, 27–39.

Callahan, D. (1987) *Setting Limits: Medical Goals in an Aging Society.* New York: Simon and Schuster.

Carver, V. and Liddiard P. (1978) *An Ageing Population.* Milton Keynes: Open University Press.

Chappell, N. L. and Havens, B. (1980) Old and female: testing the double jeopardy hypothesis, *The Sociological Quarterly*, 21, 157–71.

Clark, E. (1986) *Growing Old is Not for Sissies: Portraits of Senior Athletes.* Petaluma, CA: Pomegranate Calenders and Books.

Cohen, S. (1980) *Folk-devils and Moral Panic: The Creation of Mods and Rockers.* London: Martin Robertson.

Cole, T. R. (1986) The enlightened view of aging: Victorian morality in a new key, in Cole, T. R. and Gadow, S. A. (eds) *What Does It Mean to Grow Old?* Durham, NC: Duke University Press, 117–30.

Cole, T. R. (1992) *The Journey of Life: A Cultural History of Aging in America.* Cambridge: Cambridge University Press.

Comfort, A. (1977) *A Good Age.* London: Mitchell Beazley.

Cotier, J. (1991) *Nudes in Budapest.* London: Aktok.

Coupland, N., Coupland, J. and Giles, H. (1991) *Language, Society and the Elderly.* Oxford: Basil Blackwell.

Cumming, E. and Henry, W. (1961) *Growing Old: The Process of Disengagement.* New York: Basic Books.

Daniels, N. (1988) *Am I My Parents' Keeper?* Oxford: Oxford University Press.

Davies, L. (1978) Humor and aging: Restated. *The Gerontologist*, 18, 76–7.

Demos, V. and Jache, A. (1981) When you care enough: an analysis of attitudes toward aging in humorous birthday cards, *The Gerontologist*. 21(2) 209–15.

Department of Health and Social Security (1992) *The Health of the Nation*. London: HMSO.

Dixon, J. and Gregory, L. (1987) Ageism, *Action Baseline*, Winter, 21–3.

Eisele, F. R. (1979) Origins of 'Gerontology', *The Gerontologist*, 19(4) 403–7.

Elder, G. (1977) *The Alienated: Growing Old Today*. London: Writers and Readers Publishing Cooperative.

Equal Opportunities Commission (1980) *The Experience of Caring for Elderly and Handicapped Dependants: Survey Report*. Manchester: EOC.

Erikson, E. H. (1980) *Identity and the Life Cycle: A Reissue*. New York: W. W. Norton.

Erikson, E. H., Erikson, J. M. and Kivnick, H. Q. (1986) *Vital Involvement in Old Age*. New York: W. W. Norton.

Estes, C. (1979) *The Aging Enterprise*. San Francisco, CA: Jossey-Bass.

Featherstone, M. and Hepworth, M. (1993) Images of ageing, in Bond, J., Coleman, P. and Peace, S. (eds) *Ageing in Society*. London: Sage publications, 304–32.

Fennell, G., Phillipson, C. and Evers, H. (1988) *The Sociology of Old Age*. Milton Keynes: Open University Press.

Fevre, R. (1989) *Wales is Closed*. Nottingham: Spokesman.

Finlay, M. (1984) The elderly in classical antiquity, *Ageing and Society*, 4(4) 391–408.

Fischer, D. H. (1978) *Growing Old in America*. Oxford: Oxford University Press.

Ford, J. and Sinclair, R. (1987) *Sixty Years On: Women Talk about Old Age*. London: The Women's Press.

Forster, M. (1989) *Have the Men Had Enough?* London: Chatto and Windus.

Franklin, A. and Franklin, B. (1990) *Age and Power*, in Jeffs, T. and Smith, M. (eds) *Young People, Inequality and Youth Work*. Basingstoke: Macmillan, 1–27.

Frenkel-Brunswik, E. (1968) Adjustments and reorientations in the course of the life span, in Neugarten, B. L. (ed.) *Middle Age and Aging*. Chicago, IL: University of Chicago Press, 77–84.

Friedan, B. (1963) *The Feminine Mystique*. New York: Dell.

Friedan, B. (1993) *The Fountain of Age*. London: Jonathan Cape.

Fries, J. F. (1980) Ageing, natural death and the compression of morbidity. *New England Journal of Medicine*, 303(3) 130–5.

Fries, J. F. and Crapo, L. M. (1981) *Vitality and Aging*. San Francisco: W. H. Freeman.

Gibson, H. B. (1993) Emotional and sexual adjustment in later life, in Arber, S. and Evandrou, M. (eds) *Ageing, Independency and the Life Course*. London: Jessica Kingsley Publishers, 104–18.

Giddens, A. (1979) *Central Problems in Social Theory*. London: Macmillan.

Giddens, A. (1989) *Sociology*. Cambridge: Polity Press.

Godlove, C., Richard, L. and Rodwell, G. (1982) *Time for Action*. Social Services Monographs: Research in Practice, University of Sheffield.

Goldsmith, S. (1991) Legal, decent and ethical? *Community Living*, October, 16–17.

Graebner, W. (1980) *A History of Retirement*. New Haven, CT: Yale University Press.

Gray, M. and Willcock, G. (1981) *Our Elders*. Oxford: Oxford University Press.

Green, H. (1988) *Informal Carers*. London: HMSO.

Greer, G. (1991) *The Change: Women, Ageing and the Menopause*. London: Hamish Hamilton.

Grimley Evans, J. (1991) Aging and rationing. *British Medical Journal*, 303: 869–90.

Gruman, G. (1978) Cultural origins of present-day 'ageism': the modernization of the life cycle, in Spicker, S. F., Woodward, K. M. and van Tassel, D. D. (eds) *Aging and the Elderly: Humanist Perspectives in Gerontology*. Atlantic Highlands, NJ: Humanities Press, 359–88.

Gubrium, J. and Wallace, B. (1990) Who theorises age? *Ageing and Society*, 10(2) 131–50.

Hall, S., Chricter, C., Jefferson, T., Clarke, J. and Roberts, B. (1978) *Policing the Crisis: Mugging, The State, and Law and Order*. Basingstoke: Macmillan.

The Hen Co-op (1993) *Growing Old Disgracefully*. London: Judy Piatkus Publishers.

Hendricks, J. and Hendricks, C. D. (1977) *Aging in a Mass Society*. Cambridge, MA: Winthrop.

Henry, J. (1965) *Culture Against Man*. New York: Random House.

Hospital Advisory Service (1982) *The Rising Tide: Developing Services for Mental Illness and Old Age*. London: HMSO.

Itzin, C. (1984) The double jeopardy of ageism and sexism: media images of women, in Bromley, D. B. (ed.) *Gerontology: Social and Behavioural Perspectives*. London: Croom Helm.

Itzin, C. (1986) Ageism awareness training: a model for group work, in Phillipson, C., Bernard, M. and Strang, P. (eds) *Dependency and Interdependency in Old Age: Theoretical Perspectives and Policy Alternatives*. London: Croom Helm.

Ivory Tower (1988) *Over the Hill*. Watertown, MA: Ivory Tower.

Jefferys, M. (1989) *Growing Old in the Twentieth Century*. London: Routledge.

Jefferys, M. and Thane, P. (1989) An ageing society and ageing people, in Jefferys, M. (ed.) *Growing Old in the Twentieth Century*. London: Routledge, 1–18.

Johnson, J. and Slater, R. (eds) (1993) *Ageing and Later Life*. London: Sage publications.

Johnson, P., Conrad, C. and Thomson, D. (1989) *Workers versus Pensioners*. Manchester: Manchester University Press.

Johnson, P. and Falkingham, J. (1992) *Ageing and Economic Welfare*. London: Sage publications.

Kalish, R. (1979) The new ageism and the failure models: a polemic, *The Gerontologist*, 19(4) 398–402.

Kuhn, M. (1977) *Maggie Kuhn on Aging: A Dialogue Edited by Dieter Hessel*. Philadelphia, PA: Westminster Press.

Laczko, F. and Phillipson, C. (1991) *Changing Work and Retirement*. Buckingham: Open University Press.

Laslett, P. (1989) *A Fresh Map of Life: The Emergence of the Third Age*. London: Weidenfeld and Nicolson.

Lehman, H. C. (1953) *Age and Achievement*. Princeton, NJ: Princeton University Press.

Levin, J. and Levin, W. C. (1980) *Ageism: Prejudice and Discrimination Against the Elderly*. Belmont, CA: Wadsworth.

Macdonald, B. and Rich, C. (1983) *Look Me in the Eye: Old Women, Aging and Ageism*. London: The Women's Press.

McEwen, E. (1990) *Age: The Unrecognised Discrimination*. London: Age Concern.

McIntosh, M. (1979) The Welfare State and the needs of the dependent family, in Burman, S. (ed.) *Fit Work for Women*. London: Croom Helm.

Markham, M. (1978) *Old is . . . Great!* Watford: Exley.

Mayhew, P., Elliott, D. and Dowds, L. (1988) *The 1988 British Crime Survey*, Home Office Research Study, no. 111. London: HMSO.

Meacher, M. (1972) *Taken for a Ride: Special Residential Homes for Confused Old People*. London: Longman.

Meade, C. (1987) *The Thoughts of Betty Spital: Pensioner Activist and Radical Granny*. Castleford: Yorkshire Arts Circus.

Midwinter, E. (1990) *The Old Order: Crime and Older People*. London: Centre for Policy on Ageing.

Minois, G. (1989) *History of Old Age*. Cambridge: Polity Press.

Morris, J. (1991) *Pride Against Prejudice*. London: The Women's Press.

Neugarten, B. (1974) Age groups in American society and the rise of the young old, *Annals of the American Academy of Political and Social Science*.

Newton, E. (1980) *This Bed My Centre*. London: Virago.

Nicholson, J. (1980) *Seven Ages*. London: Fontana.

Nuessel, F. H. (1984) The language of ageism, *The Gerontologist*, 22(3) 273–6.

Organization for Economic Cooperation and Development (OECD) (1988) *Ageing Populations: The Social Policy Implications*.

Palmore, E. (1978) Attitudes toward aging as shown in humor – a reply, *The Gerontologist*, 18, 76.

Palmore, E. (1987) *The Encyclopedia of Aging*. Westport, CT: Greenwood Press.

Parker, G. (1990a) *With Due Care and Attention: A Review of Research on Informal Care*. London: Family Policy Studies Centre.

Parker, G. (1990b) *Further Analysis of the General Household Survey Data on Informal Care*. York: Social Policy Research Unit.

Parker, T. (1983) *The People of Providence: A Housing Estate and Some of its Inhabitants*. London: Hutchinson.

Parsloe, P. and Stevenson, O. (1993) A powerhouse for change: empowering users, in Johnson, J. and Slater, R. (eds) *Ageing and Later Life*. London: Sage, 178–80.

Phillipson, C. (1982) *Capitalism and the Construction of Old Age*. Basingstoke: Macmillan.

Phillipson, C. and Walker, A. (1986) *Ageing and Social Policy*. Aldershot: Gower Press.

Phillipson, C., Bernard, M. and Strang, P. (eds) (1986) *Dependency and Interdependency in Old Age: Theoretical Perspectives and Policy Alternatives*. London: Croom Helm.

Plato (1975) *The Republic*. (trans. Lee, D.). Harmondsworth: Penguin.

Redfern, S. (1986) *Nursing Elderly People*. Edinburgh: Churchill Livingstone.

Robb, B. (1967) *Sans Everything: A Case to Answer*. London: Nelson.

Rose, A. M. (1965) The subculture theory of aging: a framework for research in social gerontology, in Rose, A. M., Arnold, M. and Peterson, W. A. (eds) *Older People and their Social Worlds*. Philadelphia, PA: F. A. Davis.

Rosenfelt, R. H. (1965) The elderly mystique. *Journal of Social Issues*, 2(4) 37–43.

Rosenthal, E. R. (1990) Women and varieties of ageism, in Rosenthal, E. R. (ed.) *Women, Aging and Ageism*. Binghamton, NY: The Haworth Press, 1–6.

Royal Commission on Population (1949). London: HMSO.

Samson, E. D. (1944) *Old Age in the New World*. London: The Piltot Press.

Sarton, M. (1983) *As We Are Now*. London: The Women's Press.

Sarton, M. (1993) *Endgame: A Journal of the Seventy-ninth Year*. London: The Women's Press.

Schonfield, D. (1982) Who is stereotyping whom and why? *The Gerontologist*, 22(3) 267–72.

Seltzer, M. and Atchley, R. C. (1971) The concept of old: changing attitudes and stereotypes, *The Gerontologist*, 11, 226–30.

Shanas, E. (1979) Social myth as hypothesis: the case of the family relations of old people, *The Gerontologist*, 19(1) 3–9.

Shapiro, J. (1989) *Ourselves, Growing Older: Women Ageing with Knowledge and Power*. London: Fontana.

Sidell, M. (1993) The relationship of elderly women to their doctors, in George, J. and Ebrahim, S. (eds) *Health Care of Older Women*. Oxford: Oxford Medical Publications.

Silvey-Jex (1980) *Geriatrics: A Selection of Bad Taste Cartoons*. London: Silvey-Jex Partnership.

Sontag, S. (1978) The double standard of ageing, in Carver, V. and Liddiard, P. (eds) *An Ageing Population*. Milton Keynes: Open University Press, 72–80.

Spicker, S. F., Woodward, K. M. and van Tassel, D. D. (1978) *Aging and the Elderly: Humanist Perspectives in Gerontology*. Atlantic Highlands, NJ: Humanities Press.

Stearns, P. (1977) *Old Age in European Society: The Case of France*. London: Croom Helm.

Stevenson, O. (1989) *Age and Vulnerability*. London: Edward Arnold.

Strachey, B. and Samuels, J. (1983) *Mary Berenson: A Self-Portrait from her Letters and Diaries*. London: Victor Gollancz.

Streib, G. (1965) Are the aged a minority group? in Neugarten, B. (ed.) *Middle Age and Aging.* Chicago, IL: Chicago University Press, 35–46.

Terman, L. M. and Merrill, M.A. (1960) *The Stanford-Binet Intelligence Scale: Manual for the Third Revision.* Boston, MA: Houghton Mifflin.

Thomas, K. (1977) *Age and Authority in Early Modern England, Proceedings of the British Academy.* Oxford: Oxford University Press, 205–48.

Tibbits, C. (1979) Can we invalidate negative stereotypes of aging? *The Gerontologist,* 19(1) 10–20.

Townsend, P. (1962) *The Last Refuge: A Survey of Residential Institutions and Homes for the Aged in England and Wales.* London: Routledge and Kegan Paul.

Townsend, P. (1979) *Poverty in the United Kingdom.* Harmondsworth: Penguin.

Townsend, P. (1981) The structured dependency of the elderly: creation of social policy in the twentieth century, *Ageing and Society,* 1(1) 5–28.

Townsend, P. (1986) Ageism and social policy, in Phillipson, C. and Walker, A. (eds) *Ageing and Social Policy.* Aldershot: Gower Press, 15–44.

Walker, A. (1989) The social division of early retirement, in Jefferys, M. (ed.) *Growing Old in the Twentieth Century.* London: Routledge, 73–90.

Walker, A. (1990) The economic burden of ageing and the prospect of intergenerational conflict, *Ageing and Society,* 10(4) 377–96.

Walker, B. G. (1985) *The Crone, Women of Age, Wisdom and Power.* San Francisco, CA: Harper and Row.

Warnes, A. M. (1993) Being old, old people and the burden of burdens, *Ageing and Society,* 13(3) 297–338.

Weber, T. and Cameron, P. (1978) Humor and aging – a response, *The Gerontologist,* 18, 73–5.

Wharton, G. F. (1981) *Sexuality and Aging: An Annotated Bibliography.* Metuchen, NY: The Scarecrow Press.

Whitehouse, A. (1978) The Gray Panther rides again! *New Age,* 5, 7–8.

Williams, L. (1925) *Middle Age and Old Age.* Oxford: Oxford Medical Publications.

Williams, R. (1990) *A Protestant Legacy: Attitudes to Death and Illness among Older Aberdonians.* Oxford: Clarendon Press.

Woodward, K. (1988) Reminiscence, identity, sentimentality: Simone de Beauvoir and the life review, *Journal of Gerontological Social Work,* 12(3) 25–46.

Woodward, K. (1991) *Aging and its Discontents: Freud and other Fictions.* Indianapolis, IN: Indiana University Press.

Young, M. and Schuller, T. (1991) *Life After Work.* London: Harper Collins.

Index

AGE, RACE AND ETHNICITY
A COMPARATIVE APPROACH

Ken Blakemore and Margaret Boneham

This is the first definitive study of ageing among black and Asian people in Britain.
Until now, debates on race relations have tended to ignore the 'greying' of Britain's
minority communities. Equally, ageing studies have lacked a focus on the challenging
realities of a multi-racial society and of racial discrimination. In this wide-ranging and
questioning book, the authors combine original research with the results of over a
decade of community studies of age and race. They give a comprehensive overview of
the British context of 'minority ageing', comparing it with that of other societies such
as the USA and Australia. They show the range and variety of patterns of ageing in the
Asian and Afro-Caribbean communities, illustrated by personal life histories, and there
are substantial chapters on the challenges to be faced by the health and social services.
This book will be essential reading, both for 'reflective practitioners' and for anyone
concerned with new developments in the fields of ageing, race relations, sociology and
social policy.

Contents
*Introduction – Research, understanding and action – Comparative perspectives – Double
jeopardy? – The Afro-Caribbeans' experience – The Asians' experiences – Health, illness and
health services – Welfare and social services – Conclusion – Bibliography – Index.*

160pp   0 335 19086 3 (Paperback)   0 335 19234 3 (Hardback)

REMINISCENCE REVIEWED
PERSPECTIVES, EVALUATIONS, ACHIEVEMENTS

Joanna Bornat (ed.)

Since the 1980s the use of reminiscence and recall in caring situations has enjoyed immense popularity and now plays a central part in working with older people. Despite this fact, there is no single volume which critically evaluates the practice, its outcomes and achievements. This book aims to fill that gap by bringing together for the first time work by leading psychologists, gerontologists, social workers, nurses and community workers – who have first-hand experience of reminiscence work. The contributors take a critical overview of the field, standing back to look at their own and others' practice. They reflect on the processes involved in specific contexts and suggest ways of developing more sensitive approaches in an area of work which has seen much activity, but little reflection and evaluation. The book includes descriptions of work in hospitals, schools and a variety of community settings and will be invaluable to a wide range of students and practitioners in health, social care and adult education.

Contents
Introduction – Reminiscence within the study of ageing: The social significance of story – What splendour, it all coheres: Life-review therapy with older people – An interesting confusion: What can we do with reminiscence groupwork? – What can reminiscence contribute to people with dementia? – Reminiscence reviewed: A discourse analytic perspective – Beyond anti-ageism: Reminiscence groups and the development of anti-discriminatory social work education and practice – A fair hearing: Life-review in a hospital setting – 'I got put away': Group-based reminiscence with people with learning difficulties – Dramatizing reminiscences – Turning talking into writing – Arthos Wales: Working in hospitals – References – Index.

Contributors
John Adams, Dorothy Atkinson, Mike Bender, Joanna Bornat, Kevin Buchanan, Peter Coleman, Patricia Duffin, Jeffrey Garland, Faith Gibson, John Harris, Tom Hopkins, Rosie Mere, David Middleton, Pam Schweitzer.

160pp   0 335 19041 3 (Paperback)   0 335 19042 1 (Hardback)